Salem to Moscow

Salem to Moscow

An Actor's Odyssey

BRIAN COX

Methuen Drama

A METHUEN DRAMA BOOK

First published in Great Britain in 1991
by Methuen London
First published in paperback in 1992
by Methuen Drama
Michelin House, 81 Fulham Road, London SW3 6RB

Copyright © 1991 Brian Cox

A CIP catalogue record for this book
is available from the British Library
ISBN 0 413 66450 3

Printed in Great Britain
by Cox and Wyman Ltd, Reading

For Michael Elliott
and Fulton Mackay

List of Illustrations

1a   My mother, Molly.
1b   My father, Chic.
2a   Me aged 3.
2b   Me aged 13 at Dundee.
3a   With Fulton Mackay in 1969.
3b   In David Storey's *In Celebration*, 1975.
4a   With my son, Alan, in the BBC drama, *The Devil's Crown*, 1977.
4b   Opposite Jane Lapotaire in *The Devil's Crown*.
5a   As de Flores in *The Changeling*, Riverside Studios, Hammersmith, 1979.
5b   As Macbeth in the Cambridge Theatre Company's touring production, 1980.
6a & b   In *Rat in the Skull* at the Royal Court Theatre, London, 1985.
7a   In Doug Lucie's *Fashion* at The Other Place, Stratford, 1987.
7b   In the American film, *Manhunter*, 1986/7.
8a   As Titus in the RSC production of *Titus Andronicus*, directed by Deborah Warner, 1988.
8b   As Vershinin, with Harriet Walter in the RSC production of *The Three Sisters*, 1988.
9   Outside the tenement building in Leningrad where the original Raskolnikov slew the old woman in Dostoievski's *Crime and Punishment*.
10a Rehearsing *The Taming of the Shrew* at the Moscow Art Theatre School, 1988.
10b Rehearsing *Macbeth* with students of the Moscow Art Theatre School.
11a In front of the Cathedral of Saint Nicholas, Leningrad.

11b   In the Hermitage Square, Leningrad.
12   With students of the Moscow Art Theatre School before the
      'Raising the Curtain' gala at the Barbican Theatre, London,
      25 September 1988.

Acknowledgement and thanks for permission to reproduce
photographs are due as follows: to Lindsay Anderson for plate 3a;
the Royal Court Theatre for plate 3b; BBC Television for plates 4a
and 4b; Nobby Clark for plates 5a and 7a; John Haynes for plates
6a and 6b; Oasis Film Productions for plate 7b; Richard Mildenhall
for plates 8a, 9, 10a, 10b, 11a and 12; Donald Cooper for plate 8b;
Topham Picture Source for plate 11b.

Acknowledgements

I would like to take this opportunity to pay tribute to all the people who contributed to the Russian exchange and the host families who welcomed these unknown young Russians into their homes: Caroline Blakistone, Jeremy Conway, Alan Cox, Caroline Cox, Angela Galbraith and Donald Douglas, Diana Ladas, Linda Lamb, Roy Marsden and Polly Hemmingway, Leslie O'Hara, Patricia Perry, Lady Sainsbury, Prunella Scales and Timothy West.

Those who contributed to the organisation of the gala and teaching course: John Caird, LAMDA, Helen Lovat-Fraser, Ian McKellen, Commander Robert and Mrs Pateman, Sonia Ritter, the RSC, Charles Evans, Virginia de Vaal, Joshua Losey, Robert Sands, Helen Molchanoff, Frank Dunlop, Deborah Warner, Tony Branch, Philip Swallow, the Warner Sisters, Lavinia Warner, Caroline Elliston, the board of IFTA, Evgeny Beginin, Maria Aitken, John Wilbraham, Molly Daubeny, David Kay, John Woods.

Thanks to the organiser of the gala, Frank Hauser. A special thanks to Anne-Marie Thompson; two ladies who have been unstinting in their work and support, Carolyn Sands and Caroline Keely; Pamela Edwardes who gently cajoled me into writing this book, and Georgina Allen and Claudia Cruttwell, maidens of the word-processor.

Prologue

The journeys I have made in over twenty-five years since leaving my home town of Dundee, Scotland, at the age of seventeen have been many, the sacrifices painful, the losses suffered on the way too great and countless to reckon easily. Of course, there have been enormous gains and satisfaction, professional and personal. My puritanical consciousness – Scots-Irish-Catholic – has demanded payment at every stage.

By the mid-1980s I had reached a crossroads in my work and in my domestic life. All actors are naturally ambitious. It is the spur which urges them on. But ambition requires a context and that context can cause confusion – ambitious for what? To have a big house? To become rich? The best? A star? FAME? Acting has been described as a neurosis that with proper therapy can be purged from the system.

So why act? To entertain, of course. But it's not the only reason. *Why act?* To express a vision, a point of view? Whose point of view? The character you are playing? The author who has written the play in which the character appears? The director directing the play the author has written in which the character appears? An amalgam of all three? The viewpoint changes according to the work environment. The play or event may be conceived in equal proportion by all three – author, director, actor – or in varying ratios. I act to express myself or to express through my self, then comes the stumbling block. What is my self? The struggle for all of us is the question of finding and coming to terms with the self.

My attitude to being a professional actor has been an ambivalent one. For many men and women, the business is an extremely painful journey. Is it a proper job for a grown man or woman? That doubt hangs over us all. As one grows older, the notion of dressing up in fancy clothes and pretending you are somebody else does seem very foolish. The need to earn a living in this manner is often undignified. The late American screen actor Spencer Tracy was an example of the many who suffer acutely in this profession, finding it demeaning, cruel and embarrassing. That is why a lot of us end up as alcoholics, driven to it out of a sense of self-loathing. A cruel profession certainly, full of missed opportunities, broken promises, rejection, permanent insecurity and also, like alcoholism, highly addictive, summed up by the appalling story of an actor's demise which ends in the phrase, 'What, and give up show business?'

The question 'Why continue to act?' for the middle-aged professional actor is crucial. Some may answer quite contentedly. The successful ones might say: 'It's a job. I'm paid quite well and, occasionally, I enjoy it.' Or to quote Zero Mostel from Mel Brooks' *The Producers*, 'When ya got it, flaunt it.' The less successful ones might equally say: 'It's a job. It might lead to something, a good break.' Or . . . 'What else can I do? I'm too old to start over again.' And some may never ask the question.

For me the question became insistent; unrealised ambition and the need to be an artist and discover my 'self' became confused. It was essential that I rediscover the source and purpose of my vocation.

Robert Louis Stevenson wrote, 'For my part, I travel not to go anywhere, but to go. I travel for travel's sake. The great affair is to move.' As a fellow Celt, Stevenson's 'great affair' sums up for me that race of nomadic, restless, itchy-footed people whose need to be perpetually on the move is almost a neurotic racial characteristic.

To move, to journey, to travel! From where to where? No two scholars can agree as to the origin of the Celtic exodus. Some say it began east of the Alps, others, north of the Lebanon . . . all geographically uncertain. To where? Wherever . . . wherever the journey took them: Brittany, Cornwall, Wales, Ireland, Scotland, the West. The Americas! To the source. What source? The source of being? Was the journey a search? Perhaps . . . a search for the source of all wisdom and truth? Certainly! Yes! A search sometimes ludicrous, sometimes heroic, sometimes tragic. Livingstone the explorer, Burton the actor, Yeats, Joyce and Beckett the writers, men consciously or unconsciously caught up in the restless legacy of the Celt and Celtic mythology. The great Celtic Odyssey.

I too am caught up in this odyssey.

The Celtic journey has different forms, over land, over sea, corporal and metaphysical, through the body and through the spirit. Even into words and language. External and internal travel can, often do, coincide and complement each other.

As a child, I had an overwhelming sense of being a traveller. A common treat on a Sunday was a half-day or a whole-day tour in one of Dickson's or Watson's tour buses. The tours would start at 9.30 and 2.00. These buses were situated just outside the city library in Albert Square in my home town of Dundee. In the care of my mother, with ample supplies of Patterson's crisps and bottles of Robb's lemonade to nourish us on our journey, we would set out on our adventure, travelling over the thin narrow roads of the Scottish Highlands to such exotic places as Pitlochry, Blair Atholl and the pass of Killiecrankie. We paraded through Scotland's past, giving one small boy a formative awareness of practical history and an astounding sense of national geography.

Yet the desire to search, to explore, was instilled at a much earlier age. Primal in origin, the subject/object was my father. I was barely three years old when my father returned from his shop for his 'denner'. Woken from a lunchtime nap, I pestered him to take me with him when he went back to work in the afternoon. He, of course, demurred. I bawled. He left me behind. But when my mother's back was turned, I followed, determined to find him. Descending the stairs of our tenement and going on to the tramlined streets of Dundee was as traumatic to a three-year-old as the young Lord Greystoke being deposited in the middle of the African jungle. But the desperate need to search for my father banished all initial fears. Only when I realised that I had no idea where he worked, or the name of the street where his shop was, did my fears flood back. Suddenly I was lost. Panic followed, inducing me to mess my pants. I was finally found and picked up by the police after what seemed an eternity, unable to speak my father's name, my own name, or anything else for that matter. Years later I realised I was picked up only one street away from my home.

My father died when I was nine years old. I was sent to stay with

3

a relative, missing the funeral. When he was first ill I did not see him in hospital. I remained unaware of his illness and his subsequent death. He just simply put on his coat one day and left home. A recurring dream for many years after, in fact until my late twenties, was of searching for my father, seeing him in the distance and never quite being able to reach him.

When my own son Alan was twelve years old an uncle of mine died. I decided to take him with me to the funeral in Scotland. A very Catholic affair; men only at the graveside, women at the church hall making the tea and ham sandwiches. This particular journey was a profitable one for my son, as relative after relative pressed the odd Scottish pound or five-pound note into his hand. This developed in him a great affection for the land of his father. At the cemetery, after my uncle's body was lowered into the ground, my son broke away from me and ran to the grave, peering long and hard as the dirt and earth was shuffled on to the coffin. When he returned to me, there was a look of recognition on his face, a look that I envied. In that moment, journey's end had been seen and understood.

For my parents, the journey had begun with the Irish famines of the 1840s, when the English landlords of Mayo, Sligo and Roscommon attempted mass genocide, and the survivors were either transported across the Irish Sea and deposited into the industrial towns of Scotland and England, or escaped to the New World on the other side of the Atlantic Ocean. Dundee, whose new industry was jute, became a refuge for the families McCann, McArdle, Boylan and Cox. New skills were to be learnt, the industrial loom substituting for the plough; five-storey tenements succeeding the mud cabins of the bogs. Life was again possible, although a new feudalism had asserted itself and homage was owed to the jute barons of Scotland who lived on the outskirts of the city like so many Indian chiefs encircling the pioneers' wagon train; the wagon train being the working-class populace of Dundee. The families of McArdle, Boylan and Cox intermarried and with a new generation a new breed of Dundonians had arisen, who considered themselves no longer Irish immigrants but one hundred per cent Scots.

Elizabeth McArdle, my grandmother, was one of that breed of Victorian working-class women whose innate stoicism became the

4

centrifugal force for the community in which she lived. Her maternal qualities spread well beyond the thirteen children she bore Chughie Cox between the years 1877 and 1904. Her youngest child, Charlie, grew up under the influence of adoring sisters, protective brothers and a mother who, well into her fifties, was unstinting in her lavish care. My father's path at the beginning of his life was blessed, cushioned by the love of his sisters through a period of devastation, when brothers' and brothers-in-law's lives were scarred or cut short by the 1914–18 war. To his family, young Chic became a symbol of hope for the future, a future free from the tyranny of the jute mills.

On the eve of his marriage, his eldest sister Anne bequeathed him a small shop she had bought with her pension as a war widow. It was difficult for him to sever his connection with the mill and the banter and badinage of his work cronies. Extremely shy, my father's personality was defined by the gregariousness of company. I think he dreaded the idea of a solitary shopkeeper's existence. Initially, my mother had the burden of the shop. When my sisters began arriving, he was finally compelled to leave the mill and assume the mantle of the petty bougeoisie. The mantle hung very uneasily on him. His shop, however, became a social centre for the small working-class ghetto where it was situated and my father, like his mother before him, the bearer of the community's problems. The shop was always full of local personalities, folk whose spirit and sense of 'theatre' was extraordinary, open all hours, five in the morning till ten at night, half-day Wednesday. As a philanthropist, my father was unparalleled; as a businessman, a walking disaster. 'Generous to a fault,' my mother would say. 'Your father should remember that charity begins at home.'

My mother . . . my poor mother! The eldest of four from a second marriage, my mother had and was made to be an example to her brother and sisters. A strict Catholic upbringing was enforced by her hypocritical, disciplinarian father, Drill Sergeant Major James McCann, late of the Black Watch, veteran of the Great War. Invalided out with frozen feet, McCann was a drunken red-headed Glaswegian Mick. My mother used to say of him that he had a look in his eyes of one who had seen the dark side of the moon. As a schoolgirl she remembered an occasion when a young soldier was billeted at the house for a night. My grandfather had been on leave

5

from the front and had been summoned to the Black Watch headquarters in Perth, arriving some hours later with this young soldier. She recalled her father behaving as she had never seen before. He treated the boy with an uncharacteristic tenderness, prepared supper for him and the family and, after the boy had bedded down for the night, she remembers her father carefully laying out and preparing the boy's kit. Early the following morning, they were to leave for the front.

Many years later, after my grandfather had died, an ex-Black Watch colleague of his told my mother the following story:

> There was this boy, a young lad, frae Crieff in Perth. Wha was in Jim's platoon and he had walked back all the way home from the front and had been picked up and was under close arrest in Perth Barracks. There was a shortage of MPs and your father had been summoned from his leave and ordered to take the boy back to his unit in France. He decided to bend orders a bit and take him on a detour to Dundee so the boy could have some denner and a decent night's sleep. Then he and the boy packed up and off back to France. Two weeks later, the boy was summarily tried and executed. The effect on your da was devastating. A door was shut on him and never opened again for the rest of the war.

My grandfather had never mentioned this incident to his family.

In 1927, their respective fathers having died within a week of each other, my parents were united through bereavement.

The practice of the time in small Catholic communities was that a suitable period of three months' mourning be dutifully observed. It was regarded as unseemly for the young bereaved to be seen at social functions, particularly the local dance hall. The accepted ploy was to go to one of the local country town dances, avoiding the wrath of the parish priests and church busybodies. For this purpose, Montrose was a favourite haunt. Here it was my parents' courtship began. Here it was my mother saw this shy black-eyed boy sitting quietly in the corner. Her curiosity got the better of her, she took the initiative and got the young man to his feet. This initiative was a marker for the life they were to share. Eldest daughter and youngest son, the

6

selfish and the selfless come together, realist challenges dreamer. Such was the union of my parents.

My mother was a woman troubled by her instinct for self-preservation. 'Charity begins at home' was indeed the motto of my childhood. My father's charity to others than his immediate family was a constant frustration to her throughout their married life. In a working-class community those who have pride in their own individuality are not easily tolerated. My mother was such an individualist. On the eve of her engagement she announced, to the shock of her peers and contemporaries and the calm acceptance of her husband-to-be, her decision to go to Canada for six months. Her new-found independence, precipitated by the death of her father, needed to be tried and tested. Canada would confirm her self-esteem. Her constant regret to the end of her life was returning to Scotland after the six-month period, but her boy was waiting for her and she was obliged to honour his constancy. So she returned to a life of settled compromise.

Although she was the realist and he the dreamer, the opposite qualities existed in both. She, the realist with the vision of a world elsewhere, and he, the dreamer imprisoned by a melancholic reality, two people who had a lot to offer to the world, but not necessarily each other. My sisters were born and grew up in the Depression years of the thirties, and my mother's sense of self-worth meant that, materially at least, her three little girls would never be in need. My father also thrived in his philanthropy. He became a hero to the community he served, some endowed him with almost saint-like qualities and his generosity was well taken advantage of, much to the dismay of my mother. This was the wedge that helped to split their marriage. But there were a few good years to come before that eventuality; the birth of my brother at the end of the Depression, a new shop and, ironically, the Second World War.

One of the oldest and oddest ironies of life is how a major conflict can bind people in their domestic lives. The stories of communal love in times of war are legion. My father and mother were no exception. Only after the war ended did their rift really begin to widen. A few bad business choices, the development of new working-class communities, massive depopulation of his working environment, the destruction of inner-city life, debts that had accrued during

7

the war years and the birth of a fifth child when both parents were no longer young added to the strain. My mother's disillusionment and failing health, caused by an extremely painful pregnancy, only exacerbated her frustration with my father's misguided softheartedness. As for their children, it has to be said that their happiness was well cherished. A lavish wedding for my two elder sisters, Betty and May, family holidays to Butlin's and even a double trip to Lourdes, an attempt perhaps spiritually to stem the flow of their ebbing marriage. But my father's confirmed agnosticism was a stumbling block to any mutual religious solace they might hope to find. In the end, she could tolerate no more and one morning she walked out on her family. The result was devastating for those left behind. I believe my father had no idea of the extent of her unhappiness, or maybe he did and perhaps he was just unable to deal with someone whose life was so profoundly unfulfilled.

There was a reunion, but only a brief one, for within two years my father was dead. Succumbing finally to his melancholy, he had contracted cancer. It was now my mother's turn for devastation and this time there could be no reconciliation.

With my father's death came an intolerable change of circumstances. My mother's mental health began to deteriorate, resulting in a complete nervous breakdown. The family rallied, but it was impossible to renovate the fabric of any kind of home. My brother Charlie was due for National Service. On compassionate grounds he might have been excused, but it was clear the army would provide a stable substitute for the rest of his teenage years. My brothers-in-law temporarily abandoned their careers to give aid and support to my mother in the managing of my father's business. But her increasing paranoia, ingratitude and mental distress made it impossible for them to continue. Because of their love for my sisters they had acted well beyond the bounds of filial obligation. They had now young families of their own to take care of. Left in the family home were my unmarried sister, Irene, and myself. At twenty, she was the hostage to my mother's illness, forced to abandon her desire to travel abroad in order to look after her young brother. For a year she struggled. In the end, the family decision at the behest of my elder sisters was that she too should escape to a new life in Canada.

So I was left alone. My mother's eventual committal to hospital meant that I had to live with my sister Betty, her husband Dave and their two young boys in a small two-roomed flat, sharing an outside toilet with three other families. The strain on them, although I wasn't aware of it at the time, must have been tremendous. The last thing they needed was to have a ten-year-old boy foisted upon them. But never once did they complain. Nevertheless, I was aware that I was an intruder. Feelings of solitariness were not new to me. They had been with me for as long as I could remember. Being the youngest of five, at the end of the line, born when my father and mother were really quite old, I would regularly wander off for hours at a time, causing distress to my sister Irene who had been looking after me.

I developed a technique of conning visiting aunties and uncles of the odd shilling piece in order to pursue my passion for the cinema. The cinema houses at that time in Dundee numbered in the forties; now there are only three or four cinemas left. Between the ages of six and twelve I had visited every single one. The cinema substituted as child minder. Often I would disappear into the warm bowels of the Greens Playhouse for hours on end, watching the programmes two or three times over: James Dean in *Giant*, Alan Ladd and Edward G. Robinson in *Hell on Frisco Bay*. On one occasion, having plunked school, played truant, I went to the afternoon performance and stayed through to the evening. Eventually I fell asleep and woke up at five o'clock the next morning. My sister Irene was daft with worry.

My mother's release from hospital meant a return home for both of us. Physically she had changed beyond recognition; the strapping matron had given way to a prematurely frail old lady. The up-side of her illness had developed in her two new strands of personality, often in harmony with one another, eccentric and obsessional. Together they would rise to phobia; her worst was a fear of coal. In our tenement on the floor above us lived a coalman whose lorry would be parked outside the entrance to our close. Whenever I came home from school at lunchtime I was under strict instructions not to pass the coal lorry. This meant a detour through a close in another street that led to the communal green from which, through the back door, I would make my way up to our flat. My mother would spy from the window of the bedroom to make sure I had taken this route. Occasionally I would try and sneak in the front way; my mother would pounce on me, take me into the bathroom and give me a ritual scrubbing-down. We became like an old married couple: she would confide her doubts and fears, her loss of faith. Catholicism had been a solace to her but for a time she resented the doctrine and to me would preach open sedition. This did not last.

Before her illness her great pride had been her knitting, a talent she revelled in. After, she had lost coordination and her sense of form was severely diminished. Throughout the time we were together and my days as a drama student, she would send me various articles of knitwear which were always a great embarrassment, not just because of the articles themselves but because she had no sense of her deteriorated skill. There was no uniformity in the garments she made; she would never take any measurements, so when a parcel arrived and I could feel by the texture under the brown paper that it was a new woolly, a sense of dread would come over me. Sometimes they would be very small, designed for people with shrunken heads; on other occasions, they would be gigantic, as though she had knitted to exhaust that particular brand of wool from the shop. Life with my mother was never dull.

A new school and teenage brought me closer to the decision of career and future. My childhood addiction to the cinema unwittingly had prepared me as a candidate for the theatre. My junior secondary education was a disaster; the subjects either bored or held no interest for me. I soon realised that I would never be travelling down the road of my classmates – most of them destined for Dundee and its industries – as I should have been. I was fortunate to meet two men, Bill Dewar, an English teacher with a passion for the theatre, and George Hackett, in the art department, whose gifts were for nourishing hidden abilities. They recognised that I was a fish out of water. I was regarded by others, teachers and pupils, as a bit of a clown. My earliest playground memory was of being forced to fight a boy regarded as backward and a simpleton. I shall never forget the look in his eyes as I was being goaded to beat the shit out of him. The only way to avoid both our agonies was for me to turn the whole thing into a joke, so I switched my attention from the unfortunate lad and began grappling with an imaginary opponent, hurling myself on to the ground in a frenzy of rage, beating the living daylights out of nothing, reducing everyone around me, including the would-be victim, to hysterical laughter.

Circumstances from birth had conditioned me to perform. School-boy cruelty forcing me to play the fool, I developed a persona which buffered me against the pains of childhood. My education in the cinema provided me with an inheritance of make-believe which on leaving school I wanted to spend in celebration of the lives of my family and those who influenced me. This would entail a departure from home and embarking on a journey.

One

In the summer of 1986, I was homeless, separated, and facing my fortieth birthday alone. I returned from New York the previous winter to find that my marriage was over, 'irreversibly broken down, due', as they say, 'to irreconcilable differences'. I had been married for eighteen years – most of my adult life. The pressures of realised and unrealised ambition, work insecurity plus rejection, faithlessness and financial instability had taken their ultimate toll. I had always had, in my ignorance, a scathing disregard for those who followed the route of psychotherapy at times of crisis. I believed, misguidedly, that self-help was the only road to recovery. Unfortunately, this proved not to be the case. The need to confide to an experienced ear became cardinal. I decided to go into therapy. I had intended to return to the US but because of my therapy and the need to be close to my son and daughter during my impending divorce it was essential that I remained in England.

My time in New York had been successful: I had been in two hit plays; fulfilled a boyhood dream and appeared in an American movie, *Manhunter* directed by Michael Mann; and made a whole group of new friends. I was fêted and persuaded that this was the zenith of my career, what every British actor craved, the brink of movie-stardom, exposure to a wider audience – it would be wise to stay and capitalise on my success. Life in New York was indeed exciting. I did, however, miss my family. And there was the nagging truth that the reason for this 'successful life' was my work in the theatre, work that began in unlit rehearsal rooms in Hammersmith and Chelsea, and on the stages of the Royal Court and the Duke of York's theatres.

All my life I had been caught between two cultures: the American cinema of my childhood and the taste acquired in early adulthood for the British classical theatre – with its richness of language and plays that deal with man's struggle between his inner and outer worlds, the search for harmony, the debate of the soul. In America the great writers such as O'Neill, Williams and Miller embraced these themes with a vigour. But these playwrights receive a much wider attention on British stages than on those of their native terrain. Ultimately British actors or directors are much better served by their theatre than are their American cousins. I have been hostage to that theatre since I started work in rep at Dundee when I was fifteen years old.

Throughout the period from those early days to the mid-eighties, I felt a nagging dissatisfaction with the way the British theatre had polarised and reconstituted itself, a sense of disenchantment with changes that had resulted from a necessary revolution in thinking, changes towards a more wide-embracing form of theatre that began roughly six or seven years before I entered the profession.

The honeymoon with prosperity after the Second World War created wonderful opportunities both in artistic and scientific education. A whole generation of young men and women, from what had previously been socially deprived classes and areas, was able to take full advantage of these opportunities. It looked as if there would be a much greater social mobility between classes than had been witnessed hitherto in the United Kingdom. The universities and art colleges were filling up with boys and girls from the secondary moderns and grammar schools of Bradford, Leeds, Manchester, Glasgow, Aberdeen, etc. Suddenly all kinds of things seemed possible and, in the field of the arts, a whole new perception filtered into the mainstream of British life from beyond the class barriers.

In the theatre a revolution was taking place epitomised by the English Stage Company at the Royal Court Theatre in London, a theatre dedicated to new writing and particularly to new writing in the politically charged climate of the mid-fifties. Ironically, the initial policy of the Royal Court was to lure novelists into writing for the stage to create a previously unknown philosophical and intellectual basis for the theatre. But the momentum of the Court was so great and the climate so ripe that a new generation of playwrights without any previous theatrical affiliation was unleashed, creating a tradition of 'new realism', best exemplified by John Osborne's *Look Back in*

Anger. A class divide that had previously existed in the theatre had been breached, but for how long? And to what end?

Because of my background, working- to lower-middle-class Scottish, I found myself part of that tradition, not necessarily of my own volition but merely as a means of ready identification. After all, what was happening was happening far away in London and I was still in the world of movies, of Spencer Tracy, Marlon Brando, James Dean and even Abbot and Costello. The theatre was very much a middle-class pursuit or for people who were regarded as having a rather high opinion of themselves. These were the prejudices I had to overcome in order to pursue an acting career. I remember visiting the local youth employment officer and telling him of my aspirations. His reply was, 'Well, son, let's think about a proper job!' But because of historical timing and because of what had happened to the theatre, my entry into Dundee Repertory Theatre was unbelievably smooth.

I shall always remember my initial feeling when I walked into the theatre's green room. I felt immediately as if I belonged. The Rep was fortnightly and in the span of a year over twenty plays would be produced. The company consisted of about twelve actors, most in their early twenties, including Nicol Williamson, Glenda Jackson, Edward Fox, Peter Gill, Lynn Redgrave, with a couple of old lags thrown in for good measure. The director was a young protégé of the Royal Court, Antony Page. This, of course, was my first real example of live actors at work; so far I had only witnessed the celluloid variety. Some had only just left drama school, university or National Service, some had had no formal training whatsoever. The Rep was very much their practice ground to develop their acting muscles. It was a privilege to observe and learn from these players, performing a wide range of work over the season: from Whitehall farces to Ibsen, Shakespeare to pantomime. A back-breaking schedule, tough but exhilarating. I was an assistant stage manager, and a pretty inept one at that. Eventually, towards the end of my first two years at the Rep, I played small parts and became caught up in the same hectic routine. There was seemingly nothing these young actors could not play. Of course, there were exceptions, but on the whole the power of their individual imaginations transformed them from play to play. They learned quite quickly and toughly to be all-rounders. It occurred to me then, and now, that this range of demanding and unrelenting practical work for young actors is the way to develop and learn the skills of the re-creative artist.

The feeling of infinite possibilities for the actor has never left me from that first introduction to the present moment.

For actors a major concern is how they are perceived by their employers and the limitations of those perceptions. At repertory level, variety and breadth of range is a fundamental requirement. In film and television, and at times in the mainstream theatre, almost the opposite is true. The need to categorise, marginalise, classify and pigeon-hole is one of the neuroses of latter-day artistic endeavour. The general desire seems to be to mirror our social system; for me, the artistic desire has always been to transcend categories. In Britain, the great weakness of the performing arts has been that it has all too readily reflected the trends of fashion.

Genuine attempts to reshape the mould of our culture with revolutionary movements such as the free cinema of Lindsay Anderson, Karel Reisz, etc., were all too short-lived. Films like *Saturday Night and Sunday Morning* and *This Sporting Life* showed a poetic as well as political grasp of the shift of contemporary culture. The by-product was that it paved the way for the careers of actors such as Albert Finney, Richard Harris and Tom Courtenay. Television took up the baton of this movement but merely exploited its more fashionable aspect, perpetuating the myth of the working-class hero in soap-opera form, *Coronation Street* being the prime example. Just as the working-class hero became the fashion of the fifties and sixties, in the seventies and eighties ironically the fashion became nostalgia for our glorious imperialist past, again exemplified by television series such as *Brideshead Revisited* and *The Jewel in the Crown*.

Throughout these decades my work and that of many actors of my generation was very much shaped by these shifting trends. If you were fashionable, you fitted. If you didn't, too bad.

We have become, not only in the theatre but in all our artistic lives, bound by those subjects we seek or are given to explore and the process of imaginative expression becomes more fixed and narrowed. We set parameters in order to recognise more easily those social systems we portray. As a result, we sometimes only caricature our experience without fully understanding it, so that in limiting our vision we limit our artistic expression.

The dilemma for any British artist, dramatic or otherwise, writer or player, is the questionable nature of the material with which they work – is it stultifying or liberating? Is it possible to free oneself from class convention with its tendency to reduce the imagination? In order to liberate the imagination we have to break the preset values by which our lives are circumscribed. Some never do. Some merely negotiate with these values. The political and social burden for others is sometimes too great. Therefore, they merely work within a rigid existing pattern.

In the case of the actor this might seem extreme. But in order to act one has to be sensitive to the requirements of any given scenario, and what greater scenario is there than the one of day-to-day existence within a defined social order? So, what is required is a new kind of freedom, a freedom from the infrastructure of the society in which we live, a freedom that acknowledges a philosophic priority.

Growing up in the theatre, I was always conscious of a gap between who I was and what I wanted to be, and whether it was presumptuous of me to marry the two together. At Dundee and drama school and throughout my early career it seemed impossible, mainly due to social inferiority on my part. The notion of playing Hamlet was a far step from present reality. My fear was always of class betrayal, of overreaching myself, yet I was driven to do the very thing I was most afraid of. I had been lucky that at the very beginning of my career, at Dundee Rep, I was shown the gamut of variations on the human theme. I suppose that the experience I went through was a necessary one, embracing and rejecting ideas and, of course, the learning experience has been beyond measure.

The work I did with the Royal Court in the early days was a step towards the discovery of my centre as an actor, i.e., the source for animating genuine emotion. I had auditioned for five plays before I met Lindsay Anderson who cast me as Steven in David Storey's *In Celebration*. Lindsay gave me an insight into the whole process of 'being' the character I was playing rather than describing or acting it. He taught me how to discover the essence of the character, he showed me the traps of 'attitudinising', how to play from moment to moment, allowing the moment to define the attitude and not the attitude the moment.

The play concerned the homecoming of three brothers to their parents' fortieth wedding anniversary. It began with the arrival of the youngest brother Steven who was in a severe state of withdrawal, having only recently recovered from a nervous breakdown. My first entrance seemed to me quite simple: I came into the living-room through the kitchen, calling to whoever might be present. The living-room was empty, I put my overnight bag down on the sofa, walked over to the door and called up the stairs. After a moment my father (played by Bill Owen) arrived. The first time I did this I merely completed the actions. When I was finished, Lindsay told me to do it again, slower. I did so. When I had finished, he asked me again to repeat the action and to be even slower, again to take my time. As I was going through the action it seemed interminable. We rehearsed this one sequence for an hour and a half; all in all perhaps a minute and a half of stage time. At my fourth attempt Lindsay stopped me and said, 'Brian, how long has it been since you've been in this room? What in the room is familiar to you? What is *un*familiar? What for you, as Steven, has gone on in this room with your brothers when you were a child? Enter it again and take into account all of these factors.' Well, of course, as soon as I began to inhabit Lindsay's direction the whole world of the room opened to me: I imagined pictures on the sideboard of important family events, weddings, christenings, graduations, the table by the sofa would be littered with the old man's reading material, those awful Westerns written by Englishmen from Dorset which were later mentioned in the play and so on and so forth. Once Lindsay had stimulated the imagination – had me put myself in that room – all kinds of possibilities opened up. In the end I would get so carried away that Lindsay would say, 'Now, Brian, you really are being a little indulgent at the top of the play – there is no need for a five-hour drama, a minute will suffice.'

An important acting lesson learnt. Lindsay always struck me as a poet of the theatre. It is tragic we have not seen more of this splendidly detailed pastoral work in recent times. This was, I suppose, the first step to realising that from a position of spiritual balance and self-recognition one could begin to act.

*

17

For a time I was infatuated by the work at the Court. In all I appeared in four productions. Apart from *In Celebration*, *Cromwell* and *Hedda Gabler*, directed by Antony Page, who had been artistic director at Dundee Rep, I even turned down a part in the film of *One Day in the Life of Ivan Denisovich* to do a Sunday night performance of a play by Robert Thornton called *The Big Romance* for the princely sum of three pounds.

While working at the Court it seemed as if I were the resident 'pastoral' player, i.e., soulful working-class. I found myself caught in the middle of a paradox: I had discovered a means of focusing my acting energy on the roles I was cast in, but these roles, partly because of their similarity and their withdrawn psychological nature, and because of my own inexperience, limited the breadth of my imagination. It became very difficult to dispel the image created by these performances, and finally I felt confined and unable to be free of them. Through Lindsay Anderson I had discovered something fundamental, but it was something to be built on and the Court, because of its dedication to writing of a political or a social bent, and where the actor was fodder for that ideological end, was not the theatre to do it in.

Unwittingly, the Court fostered the actor's basic feeling of insecurity. Actors colluded with the notion that if they were working-class, they could never play posh and conversely that the upper-middle-class actor could never be really accepted as a worker. This bind of double insecurity has existed throughout the history of the modern British theatre and it is only now that efforts are being made to change this mind-set.

The work I most admired at that time – and which seemed to go some way towards the development of the actor – was the work of Olivier in his first National Theatre seasons at the Old Vic. Here was a seedbed of talent the likes of which we will probably never witness again. Among the men, Gambon, Hopkins, Jacobi, Robert Stephens, Pickup, Finlay, and of course the late great Colin Blakely. Among the women, Plowright, McEwan, Maggie Smith and Whitelaw. Olivier's influence over this constellation of stars was so strong that some of the actors were inclined to reflect the more mannerist aspects of the great actor's work. Given the power of his theatrical persona and the formative nature of his young company, it was only too understandable.

My route would not be through the young National but through classics performed in the repertory theatres of Birmingham and Nottingham and particularly in the plays of Ibsen and, occasionally, Shakespeare. But I was still in my early twenties and very unsure of my theatrical footing.

Two

During the seventies, and with the enormous wealth of acting talent in Britain growing stronger all the time, one of the first changes which altered the course of the actor was a healthier economic climate and the rise of TV drama, bringing with it immediate recognition and possible stardom on the small screen. I was headed towards joining that band of regularly employed actors who could afford to be more choosy, thereby maintaining their newly acquired middle-class status as telly actors. A social mobility had indeed taken place, movement towards a middle-class no man's land. Again, in terms of economics, because of the larger pool of actors, producers and directors could be more refined, selective and particular in their casting. And success on the 'box' meant that a lot of regional repertory theatres were casting out of television and changing their policy of having a regular ensemble to a policy of 'play to play' casting. It is also fair to say that some of these theatres could no longer afford to keep a regular ensemble. This spoilt-for-choice pick-the-crop phenomenon meant that the very stable structure which had once existed in the development of an actor's career came to a jagged halt. No longer could, or perhaps would, a young actor go off for months in rep and learn the craft by playing everything under the sun. The path of television would perhaps lead to a readier success. But the danger for young players, myself included, was that we would be most often cast merely according to type. There were the exceptions, but too few.

This condition lasted for quite some time. By the end of the seventies the big companies of the RSC and the National Theatre became more and more institutionalised. The smaller regional theatres were beginning to feel the squeeze of economic restraint. Television, too, was beginning to reduce its dramatic output, itself a victim of rising costs. The creative prospects for the young dramatic artist, writer, director, actor, designer, were fairly bleak. Also during this period there emerged a greater emphasis on the actors' political involvement in charting their own destiny. The factionalising within Equity, the struggle of opposing groups to create a more politically conscious trade union, all this was set against a background of tremendous political and social changes taking place within the country and, true to a basic tenet, the theatre was merely reflecting these ruptures.

By this time I was a husband, a father and a mortgagee. I had begun to prosper in the world of television, sustained by the occasional foray into theatre. Television for me has always been an enjoyable process, mainly because the villains – not the ones I played but the ones who ran the industry – were more easily identifiable. In TV you know exactly where you stand. The theatre could be more insidious. It was not always easy to recognise its villains.

I joined Peter Hall's National Theatre in its inaugural season on the South Bank in 1976, during which time I played in Marlowe's *Tamburlaine*, Brutus in *Julius Caesar* and in a play by a Polish writer, Sławomir Mrożek, *Emigrés*. By the end of that time, I decided that perhaps I would never act in the theatre again. The whole experience had been horrendous. The Mrożek play provided some respite, but only briefly. Perhaps my expectations had been too great (always a flaw in my character) but my confidence at times has been very tenuous. By the end of my first experience at the National Theatre it was gossamer thin. *Tamburlaine* was directed by Peter Hall and because of strikes and delays in building construction, we rehearsed for seven months, beginning in April 1976, opening finally in October and performing, in all, only twenty-three times.

Hall's problems in running the National Theatre were great. The Olivier Theatre is an ill-conceived space, designed by committee, fronted by architect Denys Lasdun. The famous drum-revolve, which had been built by a firm in Norfolk, never worked once throughout my entire time in the theatre and, as I write this, still breaks down. Hall seemed to be under a permanent state of siege with the problems that were besetting the completion of the complex of buildings. The rehearsals for *Tamburlaine* were frequently broken by crisis meetings he had to attend, usually about when or if the theatre would open. When we did rehearse, because of the rhetorical nature of *Tamburlaine*, they centred round how the production should be presented. There was a lot of talk about 'emblematic acting' and *chutzpah*. No one seemed equipped to come to grips with exploring the inner mechanism of Marlowe's operatic play. After one particularly frustrating rehearsal, Albert Finney, who was playing Tamburlaine, rounded on myself, Oliver Cotton and Gawn Grainger, who were playing Tamburlaine's three supporting kings, saying, 'Listen fellas, we're like magicians, we've gotta pull the rabbit out of the hat.' To which Oliver Cotton replied, 'You've got to get the rabbit *into* the hat in the first place.'

In the rehearsal room, Hall appeared distracted, part Father Christmas, part Niccolò Machiavelli. A common fantasy among the actors was to seek an interview with him in which one would lay down the law about what was wrong with the NT, only to be faced down by Sir Peter agreeing with every word you said in a bland, light fashion. The effect was one of weightlessness as experienced by astronauts when they venture into outer space, so that language would stutter, flutter and become dissipated in his presence, resulting in something like the following: 'Peeeterrr, whaaat theee trouououble wiiith theee theaaatrrre issszzzz' and so on.

Oliver Cotton and I created a scenario for a modern Restoration play in which the leading character, Sir Henry Human-Being, an idealist, was constantly coming to grief in the face of the real world as represented by the pragmatic character of Sir Peter Bland.

The prolonged waking dream of *Tamburlaine* was followed by the misbegotten nightmare of *Julius Caesar*. The read-through of *Julius Caesar* was the best that I ever attended. From then on it was straight downhill. Directed by John Schlesinger, the production included some of the most promising young talent of the NT, led by Schlesinger like sacrificial lambs to the slaughter, with John Gielgud as Julius Caesar. Throughout Gielgud was in a state of constant bemusement. He had been in his time a great Cassius on film and on stage and now was playing the ill-fated title role in a production whose design resembled that of a tatty tour of *The Prisoner of Zenda*. Sir John always pretended while waiting in the wings before his entrance that he was in an airport terminal. He would cry plaintively, 'Oh, I do wish my flight would be called soon.'

The notices for the production ranged from reviews like 'gang of youths mug old man on South Bank' to 'a plot to kill off the best verse speaker in the English language'. It was truly appalling. After the first night, a motorcycle messenger arrived at my house with a card from Peter Hall saying 'I don't care what they say, I still have faith in you.' By then, though Hall may have had faith in me, I had none.

Parallel to my own frustrations at the NT were the frustrations experienced by a number of other actors, disenchanted with the so-called 'director's theatre' – where a director imposes a concept or style upon the author's work, as for instance John Barton's recent production of Chekhov's *The Three Sisters* where he insisted on using the Elizabethan convention of soliloquising the Chekhov monologues which quite clearly have to be expressed in a naturalistic manner and not as Elizabethan rhetoric.

Since the fifties a debate had arisen as to whether or not the director had driven a wedge between the writer and the actor. Now in the seventies the time was ripe for a reassertion of the actor's relationship with the writer. Skirmishes were breaking out everywhere. Actors were beginning to assert themselves in various guises. New companies were formed, the earliest example being the Actors' Company founded by Edward Petherbridge and Ian McKellen and then groups like Joint Stock Company, all supposedly based on egalitarian principles, an attempt to break down the barriers between director, actor, writer, all of which tragically foundered because of a lack of coherent theory. The ideas bandied about by this latter company were exciting but the ability to identify any real aesthetic position was undermined by the taste of whatever individual director happened to be directing a production. While the group shared the same taste as the individual director the company sustained itself, but when the tastes began to differ the work of the company dissipated. In more recent times the actor's need to be responsible for his own destiny is exemplified by Kenneth Branagh and his Renaissance Company and by Michael Pennington and Michael Bogdanov who started the touring English Shakespeare Company. Their energy has to be reckoned with and acknowledged. For better or for worse, these companies symbolise the assertion of the actor's new individuality. The fly in the ointment of Branagh's achievements is that they have, alas, in the eyes of some, come to represent, particularly in Thatcher's Britain, the most formidable example of a YTS scheme. Though in all fairness, it is far too early to assess the possibilities of his achievements.

Another of the guises the actor assumed was that of diarist. Simon Callow in his excellent book *Being An Actor* chronicles the existing work patterns of the present-day actor. The achievement of this one book alone was to articulate the feelings of a whole generation of theatre practitioners. Callow re-established the actor as a thinking, visionary being. It was as though, when he wrote the book, he was the emissary of the collective consciousness of his contemporaries. For me, suddenly and eloquently expressed for the first time, was the genesis of the modern actor and his point of view. Another excellent example has to be Antony Sher's *Year of the King*, about this actor's preparations to play Richard the Third.

Three

On leaving the NT I found myself in the comfortable world of television, doing a dramatisation of the life of Henry II, called *The Devil's Crown*, which went some way towards restoring my confidence. But the failure of my stay in that world loomed disproportionately in my mind. It was only through Peter Gill and his workshops at the Riverside Studios that I regained any of my desire to act on stage. Gill had gathered a group of actors together working on an extremely loose agenda. These included Anna Massey, Antony Sher, Penelope Wilton and Lindsay Duncan. The sessions were more therapeutic than practical, a social get-together where actors could meet and discuss their fears and hates. Gill's uncanny skill was to recognise the root cause of the group's inability to come to terms with certain aspects of work. The little practical work we did do was invaluable. Through his function as a writer, he located a problem of 'oral dyslexia', our inferiority towards the spoken word and how quite often actors don't understand the simple rules of inflection. One of the exercises he would do would be to prepare a series of typewritten texts, two or three sentences or a short speech, without any punctuation, capitals or italics. The actors would then have to construct a syntax out of these words; simple skills were called into play – how to recognise a noun as the name word, a verb as the doing word – and then speak the text out loud, making the correct sense. This simple exercise made one understand the roots of grammatical speech. Out of these sessions a series of productions was achieved. I had the good fortune to play de Flores in Gill's version of *The Changeling*. For the first time in a classical text I began to feel a visceral link with the material and the ability to animate it from the edge of my imaginative forces. At the conclusion of the production I felt I had discovered a new-found vigour, but once

25

again my expectations were too high. There was still something missing. The world had not opened up at my feet and I couldn't understand why.

Over the next four or five years I commuted between theatre and television, working mainly in television, usually as the visiting heavy on either side of the law in an endless stream of 'wotcha cop' shows, with the odd gem such as Trevor Preston's *Out*, which was the definitive programme about London gangland, and, in contrast, a slightly more up-market heavy in an adaptation of Zola's *Thérèse Raquin* in the good old BBC Classic Serial slot.

In the winter of 1980, I was invited by Jonathan Lynn, then director of the Cambridge Theatre Company, to play Macbeth. First there was to be a tour of England, followed by a tour of India. The English part was rather desultory but the Indian experience proved to be a seminal one.

We arrived in Bombay just in time for the New Year celebrations. The culture shock was tremendous: I had seen poverty in my time but never on this scale. From our arrival, wherever we went we were greeted with smiles and hands reaching out for *baksheesh*. A taxi ride would be interrupted with the amputated stumps of young children being thrust through the car window whenever we stopped at lights. For some of us the squalor was just too much, but for others there was also a burning curiosity to see more, culminating in the desire to witness the New Year festivities which took place at the Gate of India, situated near Bombay's famous Taj Mahal Hotel.

Being a Scot I understood that the festival of Hogmanay was sacrosanct, it was a time of euphoria mixed with introspective consideration of the future, a festival to be enjoyed but respected. At New Year over 2,000 Hindus, Muslims, Sikhs and Parsees gather by the gate, which was built in commemoration of George V's entry into India as Emperor, and at the midnight hour these 2,000 or so shout their wishes for the coming year through the arch. I tried to persuade people not to go, that it would be unwise. They were insistent, so I agreed to the compromise that we would hire a taxi, drive down to the square and return. As we arrived, one of our number got out of the cab. I called after him. Meanwhile others had decided to join him. I asked the cab driver to wait and tried to gather our band together. Within seconds we were surrounded by a chanting mob, our clothes were being pawed and torn, hands were reaching into our pockets, our women were being groped. Suddenly from out of nowhere a group of Puttees, Bombay police, baton-charged the mob, and we made our escape, clinging to the perimeter fence that had been erected to protect the inhabitants of the Taj Mahal Hotel. We had been guilty of the sin of presumption, we had taken for granted our welcome. My instinct was to return home immediately. The feelings were of guilt, going back generations, connected with the imposing of a language and an ideology of so-called civilisation on a people whose values were neither better nor worse than ours. I then realised that I would gain from the experience if I looked upon whoever or whatever I met with cautious respect.

Knowledge of Shakespeare was extensive among the Indian audiences. When we played at the theatre in Bombay, during the famous passages of *Macbeth* the audience would let out a groan of joyous recognition, and also laugh in the most extraordinary places. When Macbeth says of the sleeping guards at Duncan's bedchamber, 'Wherefore could I not pronounce "Amen" when they did say "God bless us"? I had most need of blessing and "Amen" stuck in my throat', there would be a ripple through the auditorium. This reaction puzzled me. I then asked the Indian designer, who had been working with us, why it was. He replied, 'They find it very funny that you, Macbeth, cannot understand as a would-be murderer of a holy king that it would be impossible to say "Amen" to another man's prayer.'

My dresser, a sixteen-year-old student of Katak, a form of Indian dancing, used to watch me from the wings, particularly during the dagger speech. After one performance, she said to me, 'As I watch you during that speech, I get the feeling your body wants to move. Why don't you let it?' I explained to her that I was afraid of overdoing the speech. She then said that it was quite clear watching me how the inner man very much wanted the outer man to release what was being said in movement and that perhaps this resistance was wrong. This was a revelation to me: I had always been encouraged in the past to control my physical movements, which had developed into a restriction of them and the time had come to re-release the physical man. After this conversation I would get her to watch me in performance during the speech and always she would say, 'More, allow more.' This was to prove a breakthrough for me, a casting-off of all the Anglo-Saxon values of inhibited emotion. Playing this way in India I didn't feel that I was being judged by the muted taste of my English peer-group back home.

Until this time the two most profound influences on my life had been a couple of men who were linked by a tremendous Presbyterian work ethic, men who had worked with one another and who were visionaries: the director Michael Elliott and the actor Fulton Mackay. Their rigour was astounding. Fulton regarded Michael as the best director he had ever worked with. I certainly concurred. Both were of Scottish Protestant background: Michael, Anglo-Scottish, son of Canon Elliott, a famous preacher of the thirties who had been the King's chaplain; Fulton, born and bred in Clydebank, son of a NAAFI storesman, mother having died of diabetes when he was two years old, raised by female cousins. Michael, tall, patrician, aquiline-featured; Fulton, small, proletarian, sparkling-eyed.

Since childhood I had been influenced by my Proddy pals. They used to say the one difference between a Catholic and a Protestant household was that on coal-day, when the week's supply was delivered up the tenement stairways, the Protestant household would eke out its coal throughout the week, whereas the Catholic would have a blazing fire in one night and freeze till the next delivery. For me, a Catholic, the disorder was too much and I witnessed a few of my RC contemporaries being consigned to the scrap heap of state institutions, borstal, prison etc., while my Proddy pals somehow or other managed to keep their heads above the debris. I recognised at an early age that a system was at work and it was the system of survival, a system that consciously I adopted. As I got older it manifested itself in a driving ambition.

Fulton and Michael had worked together in London at the 59 Theatre Company at the Lyric Hammersmith and subsequently at the Old Vic where Michael was the Artistic Director in the last season before Olivier's first National Theatre Company took over. Olivier offered him the position of number two but Michael refused, being very much his own man. His desire was to break away from the inhibitions of the proscenium-arch stage and find a theatre that

28

would combine the qualities of the epic and the intimate where the audience would be less separated from the dramatic action. Michael, with his partners James Maxwell, Casper Wrede and Braham Murray, were encouraged by the newly instituted Arts Council to move to the provinces. At the behest of a group of Manchester businessmen they moved north. The first incarnation was the 59 Theatre Company, based at the Manchester University Theatre, where I worked with him in Ibsen's *When We Dead Awaken*. In 1976 the long-dreamed-of new theatre was opened. Designed 'in the round' by a theatre designer as opposed to an architect, Richard Negri's three-tiered module was suspended between the pillars of the defunct Cotton Exchange in the centre of the city. Once the largest room in Europe, bombed during the war, cotton-trading continued until the late sixties. To this day you can still see the last day's trading figures as you enter the building.

In Michael Elliott I recognised a fellow traveller. His obsession as an artist could reach zealot-like proportions. A constant theme of many of his productions was the individual's pursuit of ideals at the expense of personal happiness. The sheer scale of his effort and achievement made him the most exciting director I had ever worked with. His demand was always that we push further and further past ordinary realms of human experience. I had always worked with him at times of great creative energy. The final occasion followed a period of discontent on my part.

The play that made Michael's name and the most formidable example of his work was Ibsen's *Brand* which Elliott had directed with Patrick McGoohan for the 59 Theatre Company at the Lyric Hammersmith. I myself played the part on the radio and at Nottingham Playhouse. It was hoped that we would one day revive the play together. The theme of *Brand* is of a man striving to discover spiritual salvation and his fear of 'that' which will destroy him; 'that' being whatever each individual is most terrified of.

Professionally Michael was an inspiration and his standards were standards I very much adhered to and tried to emulate. Fulton Mackay shared this emulation with me, but as a friend advised me of the dangers of trying to force these standards against the grain of my personal and professional life. His wisdom was to recognise an assumed role that I was beginning to play, and he cautioned against my relentless pursuit of something that perhaps I was not suited to. If ever my self-will went into overdrive he would always counsel me to 'say my prayers'. Saying prayers meant simply to stop and take stock. Never one of my greater qualities.

After touring India I drifted for a couple of years, doing a variety of theatre-related work and teaching. I returned to the NT briefly for one production directed by Peter Gill, *Danton's Death*. Peter had gathered together a tremendous company and the production was a very happy one. Unfortunately, the company was under-used. Peter had promised that the group would stay together for one more production, but this promise was abandoned and the company felt betrayed. The enthusiasm and the possibilities of future good work seemed endless but it was not to be. Disillusioned with false promises, I was compelled to take stock for a time; to stop working in the theatre, to take a look at the world outside.

In my time away from the theatre, the first ever in twenty-odd years, I got a job at a gym working as a part-time receptionist. Still, I had not come to terms with my 'over-reaching' pride. The discontent gave way to observation of others. What a salutary experience it is to observe the rudeness of people demanding service of those they consider menials. My stint as a receptionist was quite an eye-opener. I vowed never again to take for granted those people serving behind desks.

In true Presbyterian style I became super-fit, running the towpath along the river near my home every day, pushing myself further and further, eventually running to Richmond and back over a course of about eighteen miles. A crazy form of sublimation.

In my new position at the gym, the people I was dealing with regarded me as blotting paper, a sop for their anxieties. I quickly became aware that in each little transaction across the desk there was a level of public performance. I became fascinated by how people would adopt a role with me, a role of aggressor if they were in a hurry to be served, the role of penitent if they were late for a sunbed appointment or massage. The revelation to me was that there were more actors on the outside of my profession than on the inside. Even in this low-profile job I couldn't get away from acting. Acting was universal. Everyone does it every day.

As a child, at the beginning of my journey, this was what I understood instinctively. All around me there were the most magnificent performances, father, mother, aunts, uncles, grandparents, generations of players performing in order to alleviate the burden of life. Try as I might, the withdrawal symptoms were powerful and the acting-drug trace elements were still in my system. For better or worse, I was still an actor and now, at thirty-seven, the acting habit couldn't be broken.

In the end I began to crawl up the wall with frustration and boredom. Then the telephone rang as it invariably does at those moments. Patrick McGoohan had decided to back out of playing Captain Ahab in Michael Elliott's production of *Moby Dick* and would I take over? My first reaction was 'here we go again' and then, 'I'd rather do a telly', and then, 'well it is a good part' and finally, 'nothing else is being offered'. So off I went to Manchester for what turned out to be my most extraordinary experience so far.

This was to be Michael Elliott's last piece of work. The swansong of his career. I felt it would be mine too. The physical demands of the part were enormous. First, I had to have my leg strapped up my back in order to wear Ahab's peg-leg. I spent some time at the artificial limb centre in Roehampton, practising with my prosthesis and watching in awe as real amputees moved about with incredible dexterity. The sheer courage of human beings coping with such handicaps was inspiring. I had to wear my prosthesis for three and a half hours every evening. At the end of the performance it would take twenty minutes before the circulation came back into my leg. The design of the production was a ship in full sail. I had to negotiate ropes, yard-arms, hatches, flying in the bosun's chair and, finally, the assault on the Great White Whale himself. Michael created a brilliant *coup de théâtre* for the whale scenes. The ship disappeared and we were left with an open stage in the round. The surface of the stage was a flattened inflatable balloon and when the whale came under Ahab's canoe, the dirigible inflated ten feet up in the air within a matter of seconds, the result being that I and the crew members were pitched high and rolled off the dirigible and into the exits, twice on Saturdays. The most exhausting piece – of – work – I – have – ever – done.

Ahab was a second cousin to Brand, and his obsession with the

White Whale again was an allegory of man's obsession to conquer that of which he is most afraid. The sheer physical effort involved convinced me that perhaps Michael Elliott was trying to kill me and I was conspiring with him in my own demise. After the performance on Saturday nights I would get a taxi to my home in Diggle just outside Manchester and lie there over the weekend like an invalid until I had to drag myself up and out for the Monday evening performance. I was pushing myself to the limit physically in order to validate my return to acting. Maybe the 'that' I was afraid of was the burden of too many identities . . . or the lack of a central one?

On matinée days the pain between performances would be so excruciating that the evening performance finally had to be delayed by half an hour. Michael himself was forced to deliver a speech to the audience apologising for the delay due to the technical difficulties of the show. The second performance ran so late that on New Year's Eve we actually brought the new year in on stage with the unlikely sight of cast and audience, peg-leg and all, singing Auld Lang Syne at the curtain call.

At the first performance, in the scene where Ahab climbs onto the mizzen rail to hammer a gold doubloon on to the main mast, the assistant stage manager had not secured my peg-leg. When I climbed on to the rail the leg fell off. Gasps from the audience. Stifled giggles from the actors, very stifled. The terror of the first night would stifle any giggle. As my fellow actors struggled to secure the peg into its harness I said with a great sense of improvisation, 'Leave it boys, let it be' and they did, the only problem being how I was to get down from the mizzen rail and across the stage thirty feet to the exit, the crew themselves having exited by then. Out of the corner of my eye I saw Michael sitting in the first level of the theatre, staring at me intently, his eyes flickering towards a rope hanging from the flies. I immediately grabbed that rope and swung myself down and, as if by magic, another rope appeared, then another, enabling me to make my exit like Tarzan.

In the interval one of the critics was heard to observe, 'I particularly liked the moment when Ahab's peg-leg fell off. What we saw in that instant was the total vulnerability of the man. It left a lasting impression.' Critics are sometimes, thankfully, gullible.

Two months after *Moby Dick* finished, Michael Elliott, who had spent the last ten years of his life on a dialysis machine, died as the result of a kidney transplant operation. His loss to me as both a friend and mentor was shattering. I felt that I had only just begun to know him. When someone close dies, the perspective on life briefly becomes crystal clear. The pettiness, self-obsession, the indulgences are seen as an expensive waste of time and energy. The need to simplify becomes paramount, but, alas, only too briefly. Resolutions are made that life should be cherished and respected and that the time we are given should not be taken for granted or wasted. The sense of achievement comes into proportion. How little one has done and how much there is to do. I felt the wish to repeat for myself my son's moment of recognition at the graveside of my uncle. I felt again that envy for his tacit understanding of the journey's end.

My experience with Michael and the production of *Moby Dick* was the catalyst for the realisation that work was an end in itself rather than a means to an end, and from this time on work would have a new significance for me.

I had been a prisoner of a fantasy world. A fantasy world that exists side by side with the real world of the working actor. Fantasy is crucial for sustaining a sense of wonder and childlike enthusiasm. Like a child with a low boredom threshold who quickly moves on to the next toy, the danger of completely inhabiting this fantasy world is you may never fully be able to connect with whatever piece of work you are doing, but always, as it were, be looking over your shoulder to see what your neighbour is doing. I think actors in particular are hostage to that world. Fantasy is necessary to feed the work, but it must never dominate it to the exclusion of genuine concentration and palpable commitment. Of course it's wonderful to be able to fantasise about what might be possible, what the future might hold, whether or not tomorrow may bring something new. The dream-like state of this fantasy world can be very comforting. But it is dangerous because it acts by the power of self-deception.

Four

Throughout the following year, 1984, I put into practice the business of 'being in the moment', both in my professional and private life. Professionally, I was successful; privately, a disaster. In work I endeavoured to be less schematic, my performances less consciously designed, allowing myself to be more open, not so in control; less the Presbyterian Scot, more the Roman Catholic Mick. It was to be two years of non-stop work, crowned by two plays on the London stage that were both to be repeated in New York: a revival of Eugene O'Neill's *Strange Interlude* at the Duke of York's Theatre, a play which had not been seen in London for almost fifty years; then Ron Hutchinson's *Rat in the Skull* at the Royal Court Theatre.

Strange Interlude was O'Neill's attempt at a marriage of the novel and the play. Lasting over four hours, consisting of nine acts, it explores the twenty-five-year relationship of Nina Leeds and the three men in her life. I played the part of Edmund Darrell, the doctor who eventually becomes her lover.

In this flawed masterpiece, O'Neill uses a technique of spoken thoughts, or asides, interspersed throughout the dialogue. The asides are used boldly to give voice to their secret feelings, qualifying or questioning the spoken word. What O'Neill explores is how the asides can have as much subtext as dialogue, that in our innermost thoughts we tell lies to ourselves, negotiate with ourselves, give ourselves false illusions in relation to our fellows. It is a brilliant exposé of the human psyche.

The main problem the production threw up was whether our thoughts should be addressed directly to the audience or merely overheard by them. We chose the difficult path of making the asides indirect but with an underlying sensitivity of their concrete effect on the audience. What this produced was a comic irony, comic because

34

of its searing humanity. The heroine was played by Glenda Jackson and with the director, Keith Hack, there were endless discussions as to whether a comic result was detrimental to or an enhancement of the text. Both Keith and Glenda felt it was detrimental; Edward Petherbridge, who played Charles Marsden, and I felt it was enhancing and only detrimental if not tightly controlled. The line was very thin but, in order to expose a truthful reality, a line that had to be trod. In comedy the banana-skin syndrome – someone drops a banana skin, someone slips on it, the audience laughs – can contain the possibility of tragedy and comedy coexisting: if the person who slips on the banana skin has a brain haemorrhage that which is funny can become tragic, equally that which is tragic can seem hysterically funny.

Treading this line was fascinating in its effect on whichever audience we were playing to. In Britain, we were aware of the audience's concentration on the play and our need to encourage them to enjoy the irony. In America, the following year, the opposite was true: the danger of the comedy was that the audience at times would hijack the play and take it where it was never intended to go: one had to have far greater control over the humour. The performances on either side of the Atlantic highlighted a crucial cultural distinction between the two nations.

But before going to America I was to return to the Royal Court to appear as Nelson in Ron Hutchinson's *Rat in the Skull* directed inspiringly by Max Stafford-Clark. I was transformed from an Irish-American Catholic to an Ulster Irish Protestant. By a curious synchronism, the play, about an RUC detective-sergeant's interrogation of a young IRA suspect in order to turn him informer, dealt exactly with the personal dilemma I was beginning to come to terms with – caught in the grip of an overbearing sense of one identity and the desire to discover a new one. Hutchinson and O'Neill, writers preoccupied with their Celtic roots and both overpowered by an innate sense of melancholy, struggle with the same questing theme throughout their working lives: who am I? who are you?

Nelson, the policeman, is living on a powder keg. The death of his father, the break-up of his marriage, the strain of his job and his perception of the troubles in Northern Ireland, his disgust at being trapped in this constant spiral of violence, are the sparks which ignite a devastating explosion inside him. He is sent to convert Roche, the young IRA man, into a supergrass. Roche refuses to speak, but after a witty and lengthy diatribe from Nelson on the history and cultural differences between Catholic and Protestant, he is goaded into conversation. This is witnessed by Naylor, a young English PC assigned to Nelson. At the point where Roche's spirit is about to be broken, Nelson sends Naylor out of the interview room to fetch a cup of tea. As soon as Naylor is gone Nelson hits Roche, thereby undoing the whole preceding interrogation and investigation of the young suspect. A CID officer, Harris, investigates the reason why. Staged in the form of flashbacks, Nelson's motives for the assault are quite clearly personal; to break what he feels is the circle of his life. 'The Rat in the Skull' is the predatory misery and hate of generations that are gnawing at his brain. From a long line of Orangemen, Nelson sees his inheritance from his father as a rat that will remain trapped in his psyche and his race.

Working on this play, I realised how lucky I had been to grow up in a mixed Catholic/Protestant environment and how fortunate I was not to be caught in a yoke of prejudice. Nelson's story could not have been more different to my own. The only similarities were the demands and pressures made by the job, the precious cost involved. That cost for me would be my marriage.

By 1986 my life had come full circle to success professionally, but to terminal failure as far as my domestic happiness was concerned. In a relentless pursuit to flee myself, I had left out one important factor in the equation: responsibility to those who loved me and depended on me. Through the psychotherapy sessions I was undergoing at the time, I became aware of this lack. I had been domestically stunted. For eighteen years I had maintained the image of the boy from Dundee still looking for domestic security. In fact, I had never grown up.

My return to England after New York, the end of my flirtation with the American cinema, my decision to stay, the need for a consistent wage packet while my divorce was underway all contributed to my taking a job that previously I never would have considered: as a leading player with the Royal Shakespeare Company. It proved to be another decisive turning point.

As a newly-wed in 1968 I had spent a season as a Stratford widower; one of that lonely band of unfortunates whose partner is working away from home for months on end. I had developed a fierce prejudice against the notion of ever being a member of the RSC as a result of this forced separation from my actress wife. I was twenty-two and my new wife had been whisked away from the portals of the Registry Office in Birmingham to the banks of the Avon. My reaction of course had been disproportionate, but the feeling of exclusion never quite left me.

I found the work at Stratford dry in manner, precious in execution. The acting within the company didn't appeal to my taste, lacking, as I felt then, any real virility. It struck me as a bit posh, a bit undergrad-made-good. Mind you, I was very young, very opinionated and probably very jealous.

When I arrived in the spring of 1986 at the company's London base in the Barbican, said to be built on the site of a graveyard for victims of the Great Plague, I have to confess that I wasn't looking forward to what was in store. I had accepted the job merely as a stop-gap, a chance to get my domestic life in order. The play was *The Danton Affair*, an adaptation by Pam Gems of a Polish play written in the thirties by a reclusive woman author named Stanislawa Przybyszewska, whose obsession was the French Revolution. Przybyszewska had written three other plays on the same subject. This one, unfortunately, creaked. But I got a tremendous buzz from working again with a company. I had never ever thought of myself as a company man and suddenly I found myself enjoying it enormously. I think what I gained most was the ability to fully concentrate on my new-found exuberance in the joy of acting; I could practise my craft untrammelled in a conducive atmosphere.

A lot has been written about the RSC. There are enormous problems in the administration of such a huge and complex company. But the basic premise of an ensemble dedicated to a repertoire in which the actor can play a variety and range of roles within such a short time can only be applauded. There is simply no other example on such a scale to be found in the English-speaking theatre. That doesn't mean that there isn't room for change and development. There is and at present the company needs it, badly. The current hope lies in the new Artistic Director, Adrian Noble. Over the last

37

few years the repertoire has become unwieldy and impossible to manage. At Stratford, the home base and backbone of the company, you have a powerful sense of family which is vital for maintaining the morale of such a group. The London base at the Barbican, unfortunately, dissipates that family atmosphere, partly because most of the actors live in London and go their separate ways each day at the end of rehearsals and performances. Nevertheless, the main stage of the Barbican is a wonderful space to act on, but the backstage conditions, i.e., green room and dressing-rooms, are depressing as hell. Nothing in the planning of such a modern building is conducive to maintaining company morale. You cannot expect people to live like moles eighteen hours of the day seven floors underground without any sense of natural light. Yet another example of the folly of sixties' planning. No wonder they call this style Brutalism! But it is my belief that it could be remedied. There are aspects of the place which have great potential. One of these is an underused conservatory on the same level as the administration offices. Without altering its intended purpose and using its space imaginatively, this haven could become an excellent centre for theatre workers to congregate.

After the Barbican season I was asked to join the company at Stratford. I was now working in top gear and felt the need to continue. Terry Hands and I had several discussions as to my involvement in plans for the 1987 season. At first the only lead role mentioned was Titus Andronicus, to be played in the newly built Swan, that intimate theatre's Shakespearean baptism. Using Titus as a springboard, the nature of my contribution to the Stratford season became very clear and structured.

There are three auditoria at Stratford: The Other Place, the Swan and the Royal Shakespeare Theatre. I wanted to perform in all three spaces, to explore the relationship between intimate and epic, the private and public aspects of theatre. I would go on to play Doug Lucie's *Fashion* at The Other Place and Petruchio in *The Taming of the Shrew*, directed by Jonathan Miller, in the main house. For me, it was the chance to create and develop a perspective to my work, classic *vis-à-vis* modern. I would try to discover the common ground where the terms 'classic' and 'modern' become indivisible. I wished, with all my experience of acting in new plays and in the realistic manner, to bring, vocally and physically, a natural and

38

unrhetorical style to the classical theatre. Not to undervalue the passion of classical work but with accuracy to sound and act like a human being as opposed to the traditional English classical actor. Perhaps I might lay to rest the ghost of that tradition into the bargain. Equally, in modern plays, to find the resonance that carries the classical play through the centuries, the relevance to our time and situation that is unchangeable by fashion.

The discussion eventually came round to the choice of director for *Titus Andronicus*. Terry mentioned a few tried and tested names in the field. I explained to him that at the point I had reached now in my career, I wanted to take risks and not play safe with an existing old guard of directors. It was important to me that I be challenged and moreover, that I try to forge a connection with a whole new generation of theatre practitioners. I mentioned to Terry that there was a young woman I had read about who ran her own Shakespeare company on a shoestring. Why shouldn't we approach someone like that? Terry, being Terry, knew exactly who I was talking about. I, of course, couldn't remember the woman's name.

'Deborah Warner,' he said.

'I think that's her,' I said.

'I'll get on to her today.'

At the time he rang Deborah Warner, she was about to leave the country for Sweden. She had worked with her own theatre company, 'Kick', for five years and lack of funds and incentive from the Arts Council had forced her to wind down the company and take a sabbatical. Within two days she was directing *Titus Andronicus*. Little did I know just how superb a director Warner would be. From the word go she brought a surprising freshness to rehearsals and a technique I had never before witnessed. Her confidence was remarkable. Deborah never pretends to know more than she does 'at the moment'. Her style is one of discovery without any preconceptions. Her rehearsals are conducted in an egalitarian manner with every member of the cast contributing. The flow of ideas is constant. Her technique is that of a gardener who treats each scene as an individual allotment, the sum of which creates the mature landscape of the play. She uses the ideas of the cast to seed and fertilise the production. She then monitors the gestation, growth and development until the eventual bloom of performance. Even then she doesn't stop. She attends virtually every showing, keeping a wary critical eye on the effect on the production of the varying temperatures of different audiences. Some have found her self-composure daunting. She never appears to be ruffled, never loses self-control. Yet at source she is extremely passionate in her beliefs about the theatre and has the discipline to carry those beliefs into action.

The energy engendered by the work done at Stratford was phenomenal. At the end of each day I would be exhausted, but it was an exhaustion born out of a genuinely fulfilled work effort and not the exhaustion of someone who hadn't quite filled their day. It is true that in such situations energy breeds energy; the more you do, the more you are capable of accomplishing. Also, I felt I was learning so much. Rehearsing in tandem *Titus* with *Fashion*, one experience fed the other. Because of the bifurcating nature of the work, I developed the ability to give each role its natural priority. Often an actor, when rehearsing a part, during the process of rehearsal travels down endless cul-de-sacs only to return to the starting point. These blind alleys can be seen as part of a necessary creative process, but also, you can waste a great deal of time. Attending to two roles at once is a bit like playing the piano. The left and right hands have to work independently of one another and in concert. This requires a discipline, the need to concentrate fully in a single direction with each hand and keep them coordinated. You develop a quickness and spareness of thought. The brain cannot be cluttered or the emotional centre needlessly confused.

Making these discoveries for myself, I felt throughout the year a growing need to share them.

Five

Drama school for me was perhaps the most exciting time of my life, when ideas were new and being formed for the first time. Because of my lack of formal education (I had left school before my fifteenth birthday, having decided to become an actor and study the necessary techniques of movement, voice, dance, singing), I looked upon my theatre education at LAMDA as a 'university' where I was reading human studies. With this thought in mind drama was the basis for a whole range of subjects; anthropology, psychology, psychiatry, social sciences, history, public relations, the English language – an endless list of subjects really. I had been taught by a number of actors as a student and they had always had an ability to articulate more clearly than most other teachers. My first actor-teacher had been Michael Gough. When I asked him why he wanted to teach drama students, he said quite simply, 'I learn much more than I could ever possibly teach.'

On leaving drama school I vowed I would continue the same process of carrying on a tradition of actor-teacher. I started teaching when I was twenty-four and it was true what Mick Gough had said. I learnt a lot. I also learnt of the great deficiencies existing within our drama schools, usually of a philosophic nature and typically about a lack of understanding of how to do the work. It is still extraordinary to me how many actors simply do not know how to read and particularly how to read the text of a play. This was more apparent after my work with Peter Gill at the Riverside Studios. You would think it would be one of the basic lessons of a drama education, but it is one that is ignored by too many training institutions. At the beginning I taught quite regularly, but during the few years up to joining the RSC, I found myself teaching less and less.

Just prior to Stratford, during my time at the Barbican, I worked at Balliol College, Oxford, on a summer drama course run by the British American Drama Academy (BADA). Commuting between performances and classes, I rediscovered a passion for teaching. My students were young Americans roughly between the ages of eighteen and twenty-four. What they lacked in talent, they made up for in enthusiasm and a genuine respect for what they were engaged in. They were a very touching group of young men and women, full of incredible optimism and hope for their future. My time with them was inspirational. Though I didn't know it then, they would prepare me for the great adventure I would be taking in a little over eighteen months, far away from Oxford.

Mid-way through the season at Stratford, for the first time in years, the reservoir of my creative life as an actor was full and I was beginning to feel the itch to divert my excess energies, not randomly, but towards some, as yet undefined, purpose.

Then came the shocking news that my friend, mentor and father figure, Fulton Mackay had died after a brief fatal illness. I was devastated. His death climaxed a week in which I became legally divorced and also celebrated my forty-first birthday. For the first time since my own father had died I felt truly alone. Fulton had been such a part of my life. Whenever I needed someone who could advise and show me the way, I automatically turned to him. The overwhelming feeling at his loss was of a conversation that had been abruptly interrupted and that we would never be able to finish. He was a remarkable contradiction of a man, a mixture of naïvety and searing perception. We had met at the start of my career, during my first job after leaving drama school. He was ever erect, sparkling-eyed, head cocked to one side, knees locked in a stance that seemed to say 'willing and ready to go'. Watching him in the days that followed our first meeting I realised that he was a great actor. The range of his work over the years had been quite remarkable. Never satisfied, always searching for a greater and more precise truth in his work. Directors would despair of his ardour; sometimes he was accused of selfishness, of hijacking rehearsals. This was never conscious on Fulton's part, but merely his exuberance for the work.

He could be a bloody nuisance. I remember once working with him in a television version of *The Master of Ballantrae*. Rehearsing the first episode, one of his tendencies, perhaps because he came from Clydebank, was to 'pilot the ship'. Steering the rehearsal, he said to me, 'You see, Brian, what you have to be is contained. It's French acting. Gabin, Jouvet, Girard Philipe. Be French.'

After the screening of the first episode, he rang me.

'Well, son. You lost it.'

'But Fulton, I was being French.'

'You may have been French, son, but you were too bloody slow.'

Fulton's care for the young artist was exemplary. His ability to inspire, cajole, bully and encourage you to work at the maximum of your potential was beyond measure. The lessons I learnt from him I will carry to my dying day.

Tragically, within a year of his death, his wife Sheila also died.

The loss of Fulton, my divorce, and the work at Stratford brought to a head the question of finding a new purpose. What sort of purpose and where it would come from I had no idea. But it never ceases to amaze me that when such questions are asked, answers do invariably follow.

Though I was unable to work at BADA during the 1987 season, I still kept in close contact. Tony Branch, BADA's managing director, telephoned me one afternoon at my home in Stratford.

'The Russians are coming.'

'I'm sorry, Tony? I don't quite . . .' Had some sort of invasion taken place?

'To Oxford. In July.'

'Yes?' I said.

'Oleg Efremov and a group from the Moscow Art Theatre are coming to give a series of masterclasses at Balliol.'

'How did you manage that?' I said.

'Simple. I just asked them.'

The secret of Tony Branch's talent lies in his direct simplicity. Many times I have wondered why our theatre is so insular and it's probably because the simple question is never asked.

Tony's route to becoming managing director of BADA had been a curious one. A theatre lover from an early age, polio severely curtailed his dream of ever becoming a romantic actor. At university he felt inhibited by his stellar compatriots: the John Cleeses and Ian

43

McKellens. His thwarted desire to be part of the theatre meant that his route back to it had been comically circuitous: the family firm, 'Day to Day Diaries'; a director of carbonated products at Beecham's, i.e., Coca-Cola, Fanta and the like; director of snacks at United Biscuits, part of a team that claims to have invented the snack food 'Hula-Hoops'; and, finally, director of the D. H. Lawrence Festival in Santa Fé, New Mexico. Tony's principle of just asking reached a zenith during this last venture. When asked to organise the festival, he merely invited virtually every single well known American star, and a few British ones thrown in for good measure, to take part. To his horror, most of them accepted, but luckily they didn't all turn up. So he escaped by the skin of his teeth. To this day he remains an endearing eccentric who rides a rodeo of chaos. A Walter Mitty whose many fantasies sometimes become reality.

Since the mid-eighties he had been running BADA, a theatre school whose brief is to introduce young American actors and would-be actors to the classics using a staff of established personalities from the British theatre. As usual in a lot of organisations the day-to-day grind and welfare of the courses is taken care of by an assistant, in this case the remarkable Carolyn Sands. Carolyn is the anchor which keeps the organisation from running aground. A mother figure who radiates assurance, she is one of a band of unsung heroines, whose unswerving passion for a principle or idea will invariably allow it to come to fruition and flourish.

'The Russians are coming in July. I wonder if you could perhaps arrange something for them at Stratford? Carolyn will give you details of their itinerary. Also, there will be a documentary and we would like you to take part in a question-and-answer session.'

And that was that.

As a student at LAMDA I played Joxer Daly in Sean O'Casey's *Juno and the Paycock*. One afternoon during our rehearsal we were informed that there would be some visitors, actors from the Moscow Art Theatre. At about four o'clock the group arrived and among them was an elderly bear of a man who moved with great delicacy. He sat down and with fierce concentration watched our rehearsal. This was Gribov, the Artistic Director of the Moscow Art Theatre and one of the greatest actors of all time. He spoke to each student through an interpreter, giving very precise notes. When he came to me he merely pointed, shrugged and shook his head, smiling. He passed on.

'Wait a minute,' I said. 'What does he mean?'

He spoke in Russian.

'Mr Gribov says you know *exactly* what he means,' said his interpreter.

I did of course. My performance, shall we say, had been somewhat excessive and Gribov was merely admonishing my over-exuberance. Later I saw him play Firs in *The Cherry Orchard* in one of Peter Daubeny's World Theatre Seasons at the Aldwych Theatre in London. This was not a weak senile old man but the bedrock of the estate, its oldest and most powerful inhabitant. When he was left alone at the end of the play to die in the house it was astounding. One saw and understood the end of an era had come. It's a performance I'll never forget. From that moment on I became a confirmed Russophile. As a student in the early sixties, I went four times to see Smoktunovski in the Kozintsev film of *Hamlet*. It remains for me the finest interpretation of *Hamlet* ever. Smoktunov-ski's was a performance of great intellect and spiritual charisma. When the Tovstonogov's Gorki Theatre Company of Leningrad came to the Aldwych, his playing in *Dead Souls* and his definitive Myshkin in Dostoievski's *The Idiot* were astonishing. The reason I saw the film of *Hamlet* so many times was also that I had fallen in love with the most incandescently beautiful Ophelia ever.

When Efremov arrived in Oxford I went to have lunch with him at the Cherwell boathouse. With him were three other actors, two women and a man. One of the members of the group was a beautiful dark-haired woman in her early forties with incredible cat-like eyes. During lunch and throughout the time of their visit, I had the feeling I had met her before. It was only when they came to Stratford that I realised this was the woman I had fallen in love with all those years ago at the Academy Cinema in Oxford Street. Ophelia. Anastasia Vertinskaya. Of course, much older, but still as incandescent as I remembered her.

Getting to know Efremov, Nastia and the others, I became more aware of a difference between our attitudes to the theatre. Our tendency is to be a little self-deprecating and to keep seriousness at bay. The middle-aged British actor's conversation is full of flip

45

remarks, avoiding passion and concern. We also have no shame about our ignorance of the theatre of other cultures. The Russians' breadth of knowledge was astounding. They talked, lived and breathed the work without embarrassment and also without pretension. It was central to their lives and therefore they had an incredible ease and grace of character. Of course they were also tremendously volatile, given to great shows of temperament. Their arguments among themselves could be very heated. Chekhov, being their great dramatist, constantly entered and exited their conversation: the conundrum at the centre of his work, the enigma of his personality, his philosophic vision of Russia's future. They spoke always with massive cultural pride.

Talking to them I thought of the company at Stratford, about how I had watched the younger members struggle with their status, how difficult it was for them to raise their perspective from merely being victims of yet another insular work experience, to that of being young artists with a constructive view of their reasons for working in the theatre in the first place. This was probably the state of young actors throughout the world.

For example, in the United States, training can become the be all and end all of acting. Working with my young Americans it was all too clear that they were being trained for a theatre that didn't want them. Perhaps a theatre that did not even exist. The chance of becoming a professional and working, even irregularly, was becoming more and more remote. In New York, taking an acting class has become a substitute for doing actual practical work. The number of acting teachers who have set up their own schools is quite staggering. In New York and Los Angeles the words 'waiter' and 'actor' are now almost synonymous. It's fair to say that New York is no longer the centre of the theatre world and that the American regional theatres have taken over as the cultural heartland – Ashland in Oregon, Steppenwolf in Chicago, Mark Taper Forum in Los Angeles, the Guthrie in Minneapolis. But the myth of New York still persists and it is there that the majority of young talent from across the US still congregates. The contrast with the Eastern Bloc could not be more extreme. Because of State support the actor's position in the East is relatively assured. The theatre in Russia is very much at the vanguard of *perestroika*. The prestige of the leading players in the major companies is high. The current Minister of Culture, Nikolai Gubenko, is an actor and the ex-Artistic Director of the Taganka Theatre. There is competition, but the outlets are more accessible because of a powerful infrastructure of training schools linked to existing companies. The danger of this form of theatre experience is of settling into an over-smug work pattern which blunts the creative edge.

So much for my theory, what about practice? I had in my time in the States given classes and was able to observe at first hand the problems. Now the idea was growing in my mind that I would like to observe the Soviet system at work.

I informed Efremov of my desire to go to Moscow merely as an observer. The idea of teaching came from him. Through the interpreter I asked him if he wasn't worried by the fact I spoke no Russian.

He replied, 'I have no English and it hasn't stopped me.'

In December Tony Branch flew to Moscow and within a matter of days it was agreed that I would do a series of masterclasses on Shakespeare with students of the Moscow Art Theatre School Studio.

Six

In the year of travelling to and from Moscow, the main evidence of *perestroika* was the changing face of the luggage hall at Sheremetyevo Airport's Terminal One. As the year progressed and the *glasnost* bandwagon rolled on with speculators eager to take advantage of the change, the businessmen's luggage multiplied on the baggage travolators and the terminal tannoy resounded with an ever increasing smattering of languages – English, French, German, etc. – and the previous nod and wink with curious slips of paper passed to Customs officials gave way to the more formal red and green declarations channels.

That first time, that first trip, the terminal had the appearance of a deserted shopping mall on a Monday afternoon in a small midwest American town: cathedral-like quiet broken only by the noise of the travolators trundling around and around, proffering one solitary suitcase to an absent Pakistani traveller, mourning his lost luggage somewhere in Karachi Airport.

My two companions for the journey were the sports journalist, Hugh McIlvanney, and his taciturn photographer colleague, Richard Mildenhall. McIlvanney was to chronicle the sojourn among the Soviets on behalf of the *Observer* colour magazine supplement and Mildenhall was to take the snaps. An odd trio to be involved in such travail. But what would emerge during this visit would more aptly fit the metaphor of a boxing match, McIlvanney's more customary 'bill of fare', with its many rounds, near points decision leading to a technical knock-out and, finally, a rematch. The bond between men that cross the border of such diverse activities is the relish and love of their particular subject. Hugh and Richard had it in spades. Our backgrounds and émigré Scots status was another bond Hugh and I had and very likely the reason why Donald Trelford, the editor of the *Observer*, had decided on the Cox/McIlvanney combination.

Typical of the Celtic working classes, we were underdressed for the occasion, me with my black brogues whose waterproof powers were minimal and Hugh in his child's blue woolly cap that when the temperature dropped gave him the appearance of a refugee from 'Toyland at Christmas'. Only Mildenhall, the Englishman, was dressed for the occasion: a seasoned traveller with a padded anorak and a fox fur hat borrowed from a Peking correspondent.

The process of entry into the Soviet Union was surprisingly swift and painless. On arrival I was greeted by a skinheaded youth posing as an Immigration Officer, sitting in his glass booth, resembling a novitiate in a confessional. The ritual is silent as he eyes you up and down trying to connect the celluloid image of the visa and passport with the flesh and blood before him. In my case this proved doubly difficult as the photograph in my passport was Brian Cox/Georges Danton and the flesh and blood being was Brian Cox/Titus Andron-icus/Petruchio. To ease the young skinhead's confusion I said the magic word, 'actyor'. He mumbled something, stamped my visa and indicated that I might pass through to join my colleagues. Thus I entered the Soviet Union for the first time.

'Which one of you is Brian Cox?' said a voice in a weary tone, a weariness that would soon grow all too familiar.

'I am,' I said. 'This is Mr McIlvanney and Mr Mildenhall from the . . .'

'Yes, yes. We've had a telex about Mr Mildenhall and Mr McIlvanney, we know about them. Where is your baggage? Come with me please. My name is Nadia, I will be your interpreter for the next two weeks.' The owner of that world-weary voice was a tall, dark-haired woman in her early thirties, expensively dressed by Soviet standards, somewhat indolently familiar in manner, but paradoxically brusque in her dealing with the airport authorities. With a wave of a letter, Customs was cleared and we were out of the airport and into a waiting car. The route from Sheremetyevo to Moscow was the same as from any airport to any major city in the world. Apart from the sleet, the Cyrillic road signs, the suburbs of Moscow could be those of Manchester, New York or Dacca. Desolation only broken by the monotony of high-rise blocks, the monotony giving way to the first of huge hoardings bearing slogans and then to the many monuments to the heroes of the Soviets, the most ridiculous of these being that to the cosmonaut Yuri Gagarin, a tall thin edifice with Gagarin on top looking for all the world like a latter-day version of the Tin Man from *The Wizard of Oz*.

Our first stop was the National Hotel where my friends from the *Observer* would be staying. It was here in a first-floor room that Lenin had conducted the opening stages of the Revolution. An example of Tsarist splendour, now a faded and frayed dowager of a residence, with its many bars, hang-outs for Moscow prostitutes, who sit like expectant dance partners at a local disco ready to sell their charms, its recalcitrant taxi drivers living off the fat of the tourists paying fares at exorbitant black-market prices, and its currency dealers, offering roubles at giveaway sterling and dollar rates. A crossroads for the Moscow subculture. But alas, this was not my destination, only Hugh's and Richard's. Their tab was being picked up by the *Observer*, mine by the Soviet Ministry of Culture.

I bade them goodbye in the spaciousness of their relatively posh rooms and drove off to the Hotel Kievskaya (the Hotel Kiev), the only Stalinist gulag left inside Moscow. The Kievskaya was located by the Kievskaya railway station, practically opposite the main platform to be precise, adjoining the open street, trains and trolley cars running parallel to each other. At first sight, it gave the appearance of a set for *Dr Zhivago*. It was snowing quite heavily and my toes were feeling a little damp as we trundled towards the hotel lobby.

Inside, the Kievskaya was packed with people aimlessly milling about. Most of them were out-of-towners, clearly not Muscovites. The floor was strewn with sheets of soggy paper and cardboard, a vain effort to protect the tiled floor from the winter's rages. At the registration desk there was a long queue. Nadia grabbed my passport and barged her way to the front, waving it in the face of the concierge. The queue showed no reaction to Nadia's forwardness. The concierge, unmoved, took the passport, put it to one side and continued with her business. After some minutes she turned to Nadia, still silent, with a look that would wither the soul of a lesser mortal. Formalities completed, we made our way through the labyrinth of the hotel corridors to the elevator, which took us to the fourth floor.

50

From there through another labyrinth to find the Floor Lady who would give us the key to my room. The Floor Lady phenomenon is peculiar to the hotels of Soviet and Eastern Bloc countries. They are a breed of elderly *babushkas* especially cloned for the purpose. It is believed that the *babushka*-Floor-Lady Cloning Factory is situated somewhere in outer Siberia, where the original Floor Lady still lives: short, stubbly, stout and sullen.

Eventually we reached the room. No bathroom, only a shower and a loo, or rather shower with loo. Two beds, very narrow and short. If you had seen a Russian bed before meeting a Russian person you would imagine that the inhabitants of such beds were extremely small and thin. How the average Russian sleeps in one of these beds is beyond my comprehension. Also the towels you receive are curious, to say the least. One the size of a postage stamp and one long and thin like an extended dish towel. How these articles correspond to the human anatomy is mind-boggling.

Nadia finally broke the long silence that had ensued since we entered the hotel lobby.

Glancing round the room she said, 'You cannot stay here. This is hotel for farmworkers. Tomorrow you will move.'

Then she was gone.

All in all I have stayed in seven hotels in Moscow, descending in order from the best to the worst: the Sovietskaya, Moskva, Rossiya, Ukraine, Warsaw, Kievskaya and, sinking to the pits, the Minsk.

Here I was perhaps at the beginning of a Bulgakov novel. Was this an augury of things to come? As I lay in my narrow cot unable to turn one way or another for fear I would fall out of bed, I began to contemplate the realities of my trip. I, who had only just mastered the English language, was now about to work in a language whose alphabet I didn't even recognise, never mind aurally understand, and my only means of communication was through an interpreter whose low boredom threshold I was beginning to discover after two hours' acquaintance. Also, here I was in Moscow trying to embrace a culture that was as alien to me as a petrol pump is to a Martian. Talk about being thrown in at the deep end of the pool!

The persistent blare of the telephone brought me to consciousness.

'Brian, are you awake? It's Nadia. I am downstairs.'

My body tells me it's five o'clock in the morning, Nadia tells me it's eight. The time difference has caught up with me. I am supposed to be at the school at nine. I showered quickly and attempted to dry myself with the wet postage stamp and long dish towel, soaked from the gatling-gun effect of the shower head. Still wet, I dressed, my shirt and trousers acting as blotting paper. I grabbed my copies of the old bard and rushed through the labyrinth of corridors and down stairs and into a waiting taxi. Nadia sits up front with the driver.

'First, we will try a new hotel for you. Then to the MXAT School to meet Tabakov and his students.'

'What about Efremov?' I ask.

'He is in Japan with Vertinskaya and the rest of the company.'

'*Japan??*'

'Yes, Japan. Didn't you know?'

'No, I didn't.' I had come fifteen hundred miles to visit somebody who had gone – to Japan.

The myth we carry of Moscow is of a lowering, brooding metropolis, dotted with wedding-cake skyscrapers built under the influence of Stalin in the forties and early fifties. Malign, concrete sentinels against a decadent influence. Yet driving through the city that March morning, the overwhelming feeling I got was of space and openness. Tree-lined neighbourhoods, in fact, broken by the occasional Soviet tenement block. A sense of faded elegance permeates Moscow, reminiscent of Paris and its vast sweeping boulevards. The Tsars were hugely influenced by the French who were, to them, in the eighteenth and nineteenth centuries, the epitome of style and sophistication. The largest of these boulevards is Gorki Street punctuated by its squares of Pushkin and Mayakovski, terminating in Ploshchad Revoliutsii (Revolution Square). It is here, about a quarter of a mile from the Kremlin and Red Square, that the Moscow Art Theatre is situated, in a small side street known simply as Theatre Street. But first, we stopped off at the Sovietskaya Hotel to see if they had a room for the *angliiski actyor*, English actor. The Russians and the Americans show the same inability to recognise the difference between an Englishman and a Scotsman, a habit I myself have picked up over the years. The move to the Sovietskaya was painless. This would be my domicile for the next two weeks, or so I was led to believe. Built during the Duma period, immediately pre-Revolution, the Sovietskaya is unquestionably the most comfortable hotel in Moscow.

With Nadia having scored considerable merit points in her hotel dealings, I was feeling fairly buoyant as we made our way to the school. At three minutes to nine, we entered. Five storeys high, located next to the MXAT theatre, the school houses student designers, directors, historians, archivists as well as the young acting fraternity. As we entered, we were greeted by the token *babushka* enshrined in her cubicle casting a weary eye over the comings and goings of the students, some removing their winter outer garments in the adjacent cloakroom. One of the great civilised aspects of Russian life is the cloakroom. Automatically on entering any establishment, be it restaurant, theatre, or even some shops, you divest yourself of your outer garments and deposit them in the cloakroom. This custom is primarily a result of the climate. The students continued to remove their outer clothes, while others had a quick drag on a fag before beginning the day's work. As I passed them, they dropped their cigarettes to their sides in cupped hands and clicked their heels in military deference. Obviously, they were aware that the *angliiski actyor* had arrived.

We made our way to the offices on the third floor, via the clunking portable refrigerator they called an elevator, where we were met by the Dean of the acting course and his Head of Education Studies, an attractive woman in her forties. The Dean was a middle-sized mustachioed man with a smoker's cough and eyes permanently half closed against the effects of his compulsive chain smoking. The impression he gave was of a barking cat. This was Oleg Gerasimov, a man whom I would grow to be quite fond of during my Soviet year. But our first meeting was a wary one. Gerasimov and his assistant Lala ushered us into the Rector's office. He apologised for the absence of the Rector but said he would arrive imminently.

The Rector's office was a large spacious room, formed by veneer panel-board partitioning, dominated by three large photographs: the customary Lenin above the Rector's desk, and facing him, Vladimir Ivanovich Nemirovich-Danchenko and Konstantin Sergevich Alekseev Stanislavski – the two founders of the Moscow Art Theatre. The Moscow Art Theatre School Studio was founded just after the

53

Second World War. Stanislavski, in his later life, preferred to work in very small and particular groups and became more and more interested in the practical education of the actor. There had been previous attempts at founding a school but these had failed. After the war, students of Stanislavski who had worked with him in these small groups, led by Vassily Toporkov, began the present school in a building next to the old MXAT.

After ten minutes of small talk, the *Observer* men Hugh and Richard arrived, looking rather the worse for wear as they had been unable to get any food at their hotel. They were hastily ushered in by a cherubic white-haired man of fifty plus. With his puckish grin, Pickwickian physique and the general demeanor of Alice's White Rabbit, this was Oleg Pavlovich Tabakov, actor, director, teacher, entrepreneur, and presently Rector of the Moscow Art Theatre School Studio and, above all, a great survivor of the Soviet system. The son of provincial doctors, born in Saratov, Oleg Pavlovich (pronounced *Alyek Pavlich*), once an *enfant terrible*, rose like a meteor through the Russian theatre ranks. He was one of a generation of artists who had come of age during the Khrushchev years, which many regard as the time when the seeds of *perestroika* were first planted, a period when the first tenets of Soviet life were being artistically scrutinised and questioned. Tabakov was also a founder, with his old friend, Oleg Efremov, of the Sovremennik Theatre, Moscow's premier contemporary theatre of the sixties and early seventies which was currently undergoing a renaissance.

From his early days Tabakov worked as a teacher-actor at the Gitis School of Drama before moving, at Efremov's request, to the MXAT in the dual role of actor and Rector of the School Studio. His most notable achievement as teacher was work with high-school kids in the early seventies at the Sovremennik which resulted in the forming of his own Theatre Studio, only 'officially opened' in 1986. The actors in this company, having now worked with Tabakov over a period of sixteen or seventeen years, beginning this work at the ages of thirteen or fourteen, have formed a unique style of work.

Tabakov is a workaholic who does a twenty-five-hour day and for whom the epithet 'White Rabbit' (in Russian '*Bely Krolik*'), is wholly fitting. By temperament he is always late for whatever appointment he has to keep. The morning of my arrival was no exception. Within seconds of his bustling entrance, a welcoming glass of cognac was poured and toasts were exchanged. His office had an air of contrived chaos. As head of the school he obviously had many commitments to deal with. His technique is to use the office as a melting pot where teacher, student, office staff worker, Party member, repertoire manager and visiting foreigner all blend and interact as part of the grand confusion before Tabakov himself settles down to deal with each specific group and individual interest. In time I realised that the workings of Tabakov's office were a microcosm for Soviet society as a whole.

Two students were introduced to the meeting, Volodya Mashkov and Yulia Menshova. Tabakov explained that they would coordinate my efforts over the next two weeks. Though we spoke through Nadia, Tabakov had more than a sneaking grasp of English.

'So what do you intend for these students?' he asked challengingly.

'I intend to work on the scenes they have prepared for my visit,' I replied.

'And what scenes are these?'

'The Shakespeare scenes mentioned in the telex.'

'What telex?'

'The telex sent to the Ministry of Culture explaining the plays, characters, scene numbers that the students were to prepare for my arrival.'

'We received no telex from the Ministry of Culture.'

And here was another augury of things to come. Always there would be a missing link. Always an important cue that no one picked up. 'Disorganisation' and 'improvisation' were the key words that best describe my visits to the Soviet Union. It would eventually dawn on me that the idea of a *revolution* happening in this country was preposterous.

'So we start again,' says Tabakov. 'What do you want to do?'

'What is the extent of their knowledge of Shakespeare?' I asked in ignorance.

'They know him.' He smiled. 'Some of his plays. *Hamlet*, *Othello*, *Lear*, the more famous ones. Of course their knowledge of the lesser plays is not so great. All those plays about England's kings. *Macbeth*, of course, they know and maybe *Richard III*.'

55

I smiled, amused at the notion of Macbeth as an English king. *'Taming of the Shrew?'*

A blank look from Tabakov.

'Petruchio and Katharine!'

A look of recognition. 'Da! Da!' he says. 'What is Shrew?'

'Originally,' I say, 'a shrew is a small wild animal of pugnacious temperament.'

'Of course, a woman. The title is the same in Russian.'

Turning to his students he muttered something which aroused a certain amount of hilarity in the boy and an embarrassed smile from the young girl.

'Your time with us is short. You must begin. The Ministry of Culture is a very old and tired organisation. We have now a new union of actors, directors and writers who have been formed to break the stranglehold of the old bureaucracies. In the future, it is hoped you will deal directly with us and not with the tired old Ministry of Culture. Yes? But we begin. Shakespeare. Lala here will set the timetable. Now you will also want to see theatres, perhaps the Stanislavski Museum and take a trip to Melikhovo, Chekhov's house in the country. This can all be arranged. Oleg Georgovich will see to your needs within the school and I will now make a few calls on behalf of you and your friends,' indicating Hugh and Richard who sat in amused fascination at Tabakov's puissance. 'It's OK. I check it.' This was Tabakov's catch-phrase in the face of any adversity or problem. 'I check it', meaning push it aside. 'Now Lala ...' he gestured to the Head of Studies and disappeared into the world of the Moscow telephone system.

After much debate between Nadia, Lala, Gerasimov and the two students a timetable was agreed. I would work from nine in the morning to two-thirty in the afternoon. Then from three-thirty to seven in the evening. Nights would be free for theatre outings with the option of working again after the theatre into the early morning hours. I then reiterated the scenes I intended to work on. Most of the great plays of Shakespeare had been translated by Boris Pasternak, but not the lesser plays. For example, in the list of my work, Pasternak's translations included:

Hamlet (*Gamlet*) – The nunnery scene – Hamlet & Ophelia
Othello (*Otello*) – Othello & Desdemona

56

Macbeth (*Macbet*) – The dagger scene – Macbeth & Lady Macbeth

but not:
The Taming of the Shrew (*Ukrashchenie stroptivoy*) – The wooing of Katharine by Petruchio

By this time I wanted to begin and was eager to meet the young men and women I would be working with. I had observed during Tabakov's conversation with us a growing look of weariness pass across Gerasimov's face. A sort of I've-heard-it-all-before look which was about to find its voice.

'So when can I start?' I asked.

'Tomorrow.' Gerasimov had found the fateful words. 'We have to prepare the scenes and the timetable and of course the students.'

I looked at Tabakov who was glued to his telephone. He shrugged.

'But you have known for four weeks that I was arriving today,' I said.

Gerasimov shrugged. 'We must prepare.'

I looked to my two travelling companions. 'Don't worry about us Brian,' said Hugh. 'We've got masses we could be getting on with. We also want to find something to eat.'

'OK,' I said. 'It's not every day you get a chance to go to the Stanislavski Museum. Tomorrow it is.'

Seven

The following day I awoke with renewed vigour. I could not wait to get to the school and begin work. Nadia was waiting downstairs for me in the taxi. We sped down slush-ridden Gorki Street past the statues of Pushkin and Mayakovski and arrived at the school. I was to rehearse in the small studio on the third floor. 'Small' was right. It was just a tiny room formed by thin partition walls of the ubiquitous brown plasterboard in evidence everywhere throughout the building and blocked from the light by heavy black drapes hanging in a crooked semi-circle. As I walked in, the students stood to attention, a practice common in the Soviet school system. At first they were hugely deferential to me. Whenever I walked into the room they would stand, click their heels and nod their heads in salute. This did not last.

Aged between twenty and twenty-five, these were the young men and women who were to be my charges for the next two weeks. Little did I know then I was to be involved with them for a further two years.

I was led to understand that most of the boys had already been through army service. I immediately thought that perhaps they had seen action in Afghanistan. As it turned out none had. The only battle scars were psychological ones. Conscription in the Soviet army is run along the same lines as the Victorian public-school system. There is a great deal of bullying and even a fagging system in which the new recruits serve the older lags. One of the students, Volodya Mashkov, whom I had met the previous day, had in fact pleaded insanity in order to avoid conscription. He had been in the army three days and on the third day 'went berserk' and slugged his sergeant in a staged fit of madness. As a result, he still has to go regularly to the Soviet army psychiatrists and have his mental stability checked.

At first the young women appeared reticent. Each exuded an aura of deep mystery and gave the impression of having stepped out of a Chekhov play. A generalisation about a Russian woman is that she feels pity before she feels love. The misfortune for many is that they never get past the pity. Loveless marriage and divorce in the USSR are epidemics of equal proportion. Lots of these young men and women marry too soon.

Over-crowded accommodation, families living in apartments where the parents are forced to share their bedrooms with one or two younger children, lack of space for the elder children to conduct any form of courtship with members of the opposite sex, lead to the following scenario: eldest son has a girlfriend, he suggests to his girlfriend that if they marry they will be eligible for separate accommodation. The girlfriend accepts out of pity for the boy and her own position. Within two years the likelihood is that they will be divorced. An iniquitous situation wholly encouraged by the State system.

It was absolutely impossible for a young couple to live together out of wedlock, unless they were of a privileged minority whose grandparents lived in dachas in the country and had also a flat in town. The grandchildren could then co-habit with a partner. These were usually members of the government or intelligentsia class, not your average workers. A lot of the young men in my group were or had been married at least once. During my time with them there were two marriages and two divorces. Once divorced, 90 per cent of them return to their parents and the cramped family flat.

The group huddled around as I explained carefully to Nadia the work programme for the next two weeks.

'I have a group of Shakespeare scenes,' I said, 'that I wish us to work on. My time is short and I will require the maximum concentration. Please forgive my lack of Russian, but with Nadia's help and my modest knowledge of these plays and your talent, I am sure we will achieve an enormous amount.'

Then came the casting and selection of scenes. This part was easy. They had already decided among themselves who wanted to play what roles and in which plays. Those who saw themselves as

59

Desdemona, those who saw themselves as Hamlet, etc., etc. As a result, I had three Macbeths and Lady Macbeths, two Othellos and Desdemonas, one Petruchio and Kate, one Hamlet and one Ophelia. To my surprise, I soon discovered that there was a star system, a pecking order, operating within the school, described as a meritocracy. Mashkov was clearly one of the leading lights. He would play Hamlet and his girlfriend, Alyona, Ophelia.

So I began. The first scene I worked on was the wooing scene from *The Taming of the Shrew*. Always start with the most difficult. It's a perfect way to set the level of concentration. The wooing scene is particularly difficult because of an accepted tradition of brutality, a tradition fostered by *Kiss Me Kate* and Zeffirelli's film with Elizabeth Taylor and Richard Burton. Having just appeared as Petruchio at the RSC, *The Shrew* was very much in the front of my mind. Jonathan Miller, in our production, had regarded the play as a treatise on the Puritan life of the late Elizabethans. This created a solid social context within which to perform. The difficulty of the play, particularly in the West, lies in its anti-feminist themes. The process of Kate's subjugation appears gratuitously cruel. For a British actress, playing the part of Katharine is a dilemma and can be seen as a betrayal of current feminist ideology.

Through Russian eyes, this view appears nonsensical. A contemporary Russian girl is much closer to a seventeenth-century Puritan girl than her British counterpart. So the problems we had experienced rehearsing *The Shrew* at Stratford did not apply in this little room in Moscow. When I asked the girl who played Katharine for me, an extremely strong-willed, beautiful, fiery, ex-ballet dancer from Odessa called Irina Apeksimova, what motivates Katharine, she replied, 'The need to find a man worthy of her.' I further asked her how she felt about the cruelty in the play and particularly in relationship to Katharine.

She said, 'Life is cruel.'

Western women see the play as shocking. But to a woman from the East, it merely reflects a brutal aspect of her own life. Petruchio constantly reminds Katharine that the world they both live in is a patriarchy which she in particular is forced to accept, whether she likes it or not. If she fights back it will cast her out, destroy her. The realities are harsh, but then, as the eldest daughter Katharine is regarded by her father as a valuable pawn in a property game between seller and buyer. The only possible escape for Katharine and Petruchio is to create a world where the sun and moon are seen as indistinguishable, where together they can freely alter man's accepted perceptions. A private world which they mutually create, a world of their own in which they build a future. The play can no longer be regarded as a simple comedy, but as a dark problem play.

Russia, too, is a strict patriarchy, a society where women are not treated equally even though there appear to be equalities, particularly in work and labour. But the women, though spiritually stronger, are still at the beck and call of men. Sad, tragic, but true.

As a result, I was able to take the idea of the subversive caring of Petruchio for Katharine much further. Also Katharine's shrewishness had a greater reality and was rooted in a desire for love, love that she failed to receive from her father. Petruchio was played by Sergei Shentalinski, a stocky, compact, eager young man whose optimistic personality would prove a source of confidence and constancy to me during my many visits to Moscow. His was the first of the student voices to attempt to breach the English language barrier. That first morning, when the intrepid chroniclers from the *Observer* entered the perilously frozen lift, he turned to them and remarked in perfect English, 'Beautiful Soviet system.'

Sergei was loved and respected by most of his fellow students, a young man with a heart as large as the Caspian Sea. His concentration in rehearsals was total. Both he and Apeksimova grasped the prickly nettle of the scene in both their hands. Within a matter of days they blended the subtleties of the comic and serious aspects of the scene, adding a great delicacy and idiosyncratic virtuosity. It was exciting to witness the difference between these supple young Russian student actors and their sometimes stiff British contemporaries. Because of their uninhibited physicality, they seemed to have a much more heightened awareness of how their bodies behaved. The men especially allow a natural femininity and grace to show through in their every movement. They were neither embarrassed nor reserved about their physical behaviour.

The question of physicality arose again in the *Othello* scenes. The students were under the misconception that in Shakespeare there should be no physical contact between the sexes; a precept no doubt introduced by Russian theatreologists to curb the natural exuberance of the indigenous performer and preserve a classical grace. I soon disabused them of this theory. For me the physical rhythm of Shakespeare provides a complete symmetry to the music of his verse.

In *Othello*, in the scene where Desdemona tries to persuade the Moor to bring Cassio back into favour, the intention of the actor requires her to play her part with charm, unselfconscious sexuality and a relaxed sensual ease. What we see in the scene is a young girl who is married to this old man and how deeply infatuated he is with her. Unwittingly in the scene, Desdemona, through her uninhibited familiarity, is storing up trouble for herself. Othello becomes putty in her hands and from being unselfconscious of the effect she is having upon him, suddenly, for a brief second, she is aware of the true nature of her power. The rhythm of the scene describes its physical nature, for example, in her reiteration of the time when Othello will see Cassio again. Her urging petulant questions drive the scene forwards almost physically as she clings to the Moor until he answers:

DESDEMONA ... Good my love, call him back.
OTHELLO   Not now, sweet Desdemona; some other time.
DESDEMONA But shall it be shortly?
OTHELLO   The sooner sweet for you.
DESDEMONA Shall it be tonight at supper?
OTHELLO   No, not tonight.
DESDEMONA Tomorrow dinner then?
OTHELLO   I shall not dine at home;
           I meet the captains in the citadel.
DESDEMONA Why then, tomorrow night or Tuesday morn,
           On Tuesday noon or night, on Wednesday morn,
           I prithee name the time; but let it not
           Exceed three days. I'faith he is penitent.

and so on until, finally, Othello is overcome by her charming insistence.

OTHELLO   Prithee no more. Let him come when he will.
           I will deny thee nothing.

and repeats later with a plea:

> OTHELLO   I will deny thee nothing.
> Whereon I do beseech thee grant me this,
> To leave me but a little to myself.

and then Desdemona, in an instant, coyly realising her power says:

> DESDEMONA Shall I deny you?

and at this point, there should be a beat before she continues. In that beat, just for a second, she plays with the tiger of Othello's emotions. She continues:

> DESDEMONA No; farewell my lord.
> OTHELLO   Farewell, my Desdemona. I'll come to thee straight.

Desdemona exits. Othello is left to contemplate his relationship, a man besotted, head over heels in love.

> OTHELLO   Excellent wretch! Perdition catch my soul,
> But I do love thee; and when I love thee not
> Chaos is come again.

Now Othello understands fully the extremity of his feelings, now at the peak of his passion and at the point from which he will fall to the depths of despair.

In setting the scene for the students, I created a work situation between Iago and Othello which Desdemona interrupted. There are a myriad possibilities for this setting. Othello at a desk, working with maps on the floor, reading reports, dictating letters, etc., etc. I allowed the students the freedom to create the scene in whatever way best served them, but also encouraged Desdemona to explore the full possibilities of physical persuasiveness in order to get Othello to reinstate Cassio. The results were fascinating. Each girl chose a slightly different route. One removed a pen from Othello's hand and played with it. The other manoeuvred a series of cushions on the floor set to illustrate Othello's Arab background. By manoeuvring these cushions, she gently undermined and moved him both figuratively in the words and literally by the physical act. The result gave a humorous playful edge to the scene. The girl who removed the pen flung herself in exasperation full length across the table gazing up into Othello's eyes in order to fix his attention. It brought to mind the forties' song 'Baby It's Cold Outside'.

What was demonstrated by these young actors, because of their training, was the ability to use their imaginations with infinite variety, never forgetting the basic action of a scene: i.e., intention and objective, where the scene was heading, what they had to achieve and why a character perhaps would not achieve his objective but lose out. Sometimes their attentiveness to these details would lapse, which was ironic working in Stanislavski's own backyard, when they ignored one of the basic tenets of his teaching by neglecting the pre-life of a scene, failing to realise themselves fully before they stepped into it. But then I had to remember they were still students and not yet professionals.

The great discovery at the end of my first three days, whilst I had been working with these kids in English and they performed in Russian, was that never once did I sense a language barrier. Nadia of course had helped in translating the detailed breaking down of the text. But what we had achieved together in an incredibly short time was an understanding on an intuitive physical level that went beyond language. It is the way babies and animals understand by facial expression, sound and the nuances of inflexion, by the merest lift of an eyebrow or gesture of a hand, all these means of communication coming into play when spoken language is unavailable. Or as when one of our senses is deprived and the other senses compensate. We had created our own language. Of course in time, I began to learn the odd Russian phrase or word, particularly those used in the theatre such as: *plokho* (bad); *khorosho* (good); *tochka* (fullstop); *nachinat* (begin), and my personal favourite, *yeshcho raz* (once more).

At the end of three days I was summoned to meet a Mr Shulukov at the Ministry of Culture. Mr Shulukov was the gentleman who had officially invited me to the USSR. I dutifully arrived at the MoC offices in the fashionable Arbat district of Moscow. The conversation consisted mainly of a drawn-out repetitious apology about the hotel situation and the fact that the cultural departments carried very little influence compared to the sciences, trade or politics, when it came to the allocation of accommodation. Also that March was the month of conventions for the collective farms and endless trade delegations. Not a good month for the arts. They had no knowledge of my telexes, hoped that I was happy at the Sovietskaya Hotel and unfortunately, I would have to move once again towards the end of my visit, perhaps to the Varshava (Warsaw) Hotel. Not one word was mentioned about the students, the MXAT, or the nature of my work. Nadia sat in cynical silence.

As we left the Embassy she turned to me and said, 'Why do you bother with these people? They are so boring. They can do nothing but issue travel passes.' Nadia was a lady who had seen it all before.

After our visit to the bureaucrats and with some time on our hands, Nadia thought perhaps I would like to do some shopping for souvenirs. Nothing had been further from my mind. But I was intrigued to see for myself the quality of goods in the shops, having seen so much in our media back home about poor quality, long queues and food shortages. This was not the kind of shopping that Nadia intended. She hailed a taxi which drove us to a location along the Moscow river just behind the Mezh, the International Trade Centre, where the road ended in a cul-de-sac opening on to a huge car park. By this car park there was an inconspicuous building.

On entering I got the shock of my life. Before me were rows and rows of differing brands of vodka, Russian brandy, Havana cigars, foodstuffs, Beluga caviar, a sumptuous supply beyond the dreams of your average Muscovite. I could not believe my eyes. Nadia explained that this was the *beriozka* of *beriozkas*. There are *beriozka* shops in most of the top hotels. The only form of payment accepted in these shops is 'hard currency', i.e., anything but the rouble; credit cards, sterling and, most sought after, the dollar. These shops usually supply what is euphemistically described in the travel books as a 'relatively wide range of consumer goods and stuff not found in the general run of shops'. This particular *beriozka* epitomised a massive understatement of the Moscow Baedeker. Nadia further explained that this store was for the benefit of diplomats and all credit-card holders. I observed that there were a number of Soviets using these stores. When I questioned Nadia about this, she merely smiled and said, 'Probably they work in the embassies.'

My compatriots from the *Observer* were equally taken aback by this spectacle, though perhaps grateful, as finding edible food during our first week was almost impossible.

On our first night, we had been recommended a restaurant called the Baku, scene of many a culinary struggle. The most recognisable dish on the menu was chicken pilaf. The chicken gave the appearance, on the evidence of what I imagined was its leg, of having been frightened to death by the news of Chernobyl. The rice was curiously sweet. Vegetables are always scarce and, from observation of another table, we noticed a dish of what looked like pickles. Pickles they were, but pickled in paraffin. Moscow is a vegetarian's nightmare. Richard, our photographer, was I believe vegetarian, or quite near. We feared that he might starve to death before the end of our visit. Each day he became paler and paler, thinner and thinner, but was eventually rescued by the fruit from the *beriozka*.

Eight

Throughout that first week in Moscow I settled into a routine of work. At the weekend I would travel to Leningrad. Before then there would be visits to the theatre. Tabakov arranged our first outing which was to the Ermolova Theatre to see a contemporary play, *The Sporting Scenes of 1981*. Using the Muscovite craze for jogging as its theme, the play dealt with two couples and their interaction during their routine weekend jog, a kind of *Who's Afraid of Virginia Woolf?* Russian style. The production, apart from the fine acting, had all the worst excesses of Soviet theatre and an over-elaborate design for what was quite a simple idea. What I thought interesting to note was the audience's reaction. The play was received in silence, with occasional muted laughter. The theatre was packed and it was clear it was a box-office winner. It was one of the first commercial contemporary plays to deal with domestic issues on the Moscow stage for some time. Not particularly admired among the theatre community of Moscow, it was hugely popular with audiences.

Our next excursion was to see the Theatre of Young Spectators' performance of Bulgakov's *Heart of a Dog*. Again, it was over-produced by the female director, Generietta Yanovskaya. The play is a masterful allegory of Stalinism. It centres round the story of a scientist/doctor who transplants the hormones and heart of a dead convict into the body of a dog. The actor Alexander Vdovin playing both dog and convict, was brilliant. This performance marked his return to the theatre after an absence of eight years. Vdovin had previously worked at the Theatre of Young Spectators, but had got himself into political trouble with the State and as a result was dismissed from the theatre and had been working, during his banishment, as a refuse collector.

The director Yanovskaya, regarded as a radical, was herself a victim

67

of the authorities. She had only just, after a long career in enforced obscurity, taken over as Artistic Director. One of her first tasks was to reinstate Vdovin to his proper position within the company. Clearly, he was head and shoulders above the rest of the cast, some of whom had been with the company too long. There was a wonderful piece of stage business revolving around a scientist/doctor obsessed with the music of Verdi, particularly *Aïda*: at various intervals throughout the evening inexplicably the stage would be swamped by a bunch of Egyptians in full exotic dress.

This notion of fixing on an obscure tangential image is a recurring mannerism among theatrical productions in the Eastern Bloc. The exception to this, and perhaps the finest theatre I saw in Moscow, was the work of Tabakov himself at his studio theatre. The first play I saw in this space was his production of Neil Simon's *Biloxi Blues*. Using a simple unit motif of bunk beds, the production had a great fluidity. The bunks served as a troop train, a dormitory and a brothel. The precision of the playing of the young cast was dazzling. These young performers played at a very high energy level, employing incredible powers of ensemble concentration with great wit and invention. Their timing was reminiscent of the most brilliant trapeze artists, depending on one another for the perfectly timed catch one hundred and fifty feet up in the air, without a net.

With a seating capacity of about one hundred, the theatre space is corridor-shaped, divided absolutely equally between actor and audience. The effect is of looking through a kaleidoscope. It succeeds in supporting a changing repertoire system, which, considering the space, is remarkable. Apart from the theatre the studio has rehearsal space, a gallery and offices. Its 'official opening' in 1986 marked the beginning of *perestroika* and it has received a regular subsidy ever since.

In general, theatre in Moscow is integral to the social life of the Muscovite. Theatres are regularly full and though the prices of admission are reasonable, three roubles, there is still a thriving black market for seats. The success of a play depends not on Michael Billington, John Peter or Frank Rich, but on word of mouth. The collective consciousness of the Moscow theatre-going public historically has always been the major arbiter of success and failure. Chekhov's debut with *The Seagull* was panned by the literati, but the second production at the MXAT was supported by an audience eager for new work.

One by one myths were being dispelled, myths that had been held up to me as a young man about the nature of Soviet life and theatre. First, the notion that the theatre was non-political. I was discovering the contrary. Aesthetics of course are of prime importance in Soviet theatre art, but equally the philosophy of politics has always been present, usually in the guise of allegory; a powerful history of a vibrant political theatre set against the background of repression – Tsarist in the nineteenth century, Stalinist in the twentieth. Allegory and satire are key weapons of Soviet painting, literature and the theatre. Gogol, Levitan, Chekhov, Bulgakov and, at present, Alexanders Galin and Gelman.

The contrast between the interplay of aesthetic and political theatre of the Soviets emphasises the paucity of the simplistic agitprop tradition among some of our modern British dramatists.

A major fault of Soviet theatre is an over-reverential respect for the *auteur*, the director as guru and conceptualiser. A common feature of rehearsals of the great directors was to have a group of critics and theatreologists sitting in attendance. A story is told of the director, Efros, that when the great man had apparently elicited a piece of business from an actor, the assembled scribes would burst into applause. The great man would turn and accept his applause with a slight bow. A situation that would not be tolerated in England, one of the healthier aspects of our theatre I think. The director's 'concept' was very much prevalent in a great deal of the Russian work and was sometimes too stifling for words. Yet the overall impression was that this was the greatest acting I had ever seen.

The Russian actor is a magnificent combination of the effortlessness of the best American and French film actors and the classical bravura and clarity of the best British stage actors. He avoids the indulgent and undisciplined weaknesses of some American actors and the caricatured indicating of the English. When a great Russian actor moves on stage, his body carries a history with a huge centre of gravity that is profound, yet poetic. In ensemble, their playing together has the familiarity of people who have known each other for a long time and are sensitive to the nuances of their partners. For me this reflected the best aspects of the work at the RSC, a company brought together for only two years, at the end of which their familiarity of playing together ripened and deepened the work of the whole ensemble. There is of course always the danger of complacency with companies that have been together for too many years, a self-satisfaction sets in, a smugness emerges in the playing.

One of the finest examples of playing at this level of freshness and excitement was to be found at the MXAT. Oleg Borisov was one of the other players who had visited Oxford with Efremov. I had watched him in class play a piece from *Uncle Vanya*, the map scene, in which he played the doctor Astrov. Astrov, frankly, was not Borisov's part, but his sense of living in the moment and the completeness of the man made one forget that the actor playing him looked in real life like your average bank manager. Borisov has an ordinariness which he translates to the stage and then elevates into a vivid reality. At the MXAT I saw him in Dostoievski's *Krotkaya* ('The Meek One'), virtually a monologue, in which he played an old pawnbroker who marries a girl young enough to be his granddaughter. The girl is in the state of 'krotkaya', which in English is difficult to translate, but roughly means a combination of aimlessness, melancholy, and inner stubbornness. The pawnbroker becomes obsessed with his young wife and in the course of the play she commits suicide. Borisov's performance was monumental. This mild-mannered fellow from Leningrad transformed himself into a taut, possessed figure. His was some of the most stunning acting I have ever seen.

The most moving aspect of this production, directed by Lev Dodin from the Maly Theatre in Leningrad, was its effect on its audience. I have never seen an audience so completely engrossed by a piece of work. When the climax of the play came, they erupted into an ecstasy of applause and the usual flowers showered the stage. A unique experience made more so by the fact that it was an adaptation of a minor short story of Dostoievski into a chamber piece for two actors and presented in a thousand-seat theatre. Not one seat was empty. It is inconceivable to think of an exact British equivalent. Perhaps if you imagine a Thomas Hardy short story for two actors which then fills the Barbican Theatre. Sitting in that auditorium you sensed that every member of the audience knew this story and felt it to be part of their cultural heritage. I doubt I would feel the same at

70

the Barbican. The fact is that in a society where the inhabitants have suffered severe repression, censorship and the most frightening sensory deprivation for well over seventy years, the average member of that audience is better read by far than his British or American counterpart.

To paraphrase Arthur Miller, the Soviet audiences are better rehearsed. And the reason is the availability of theatre to the masses due to State subsidy. In Britain, the shrinking subsidy has meant increasing ticket prices which in turn means that only a minority can afford to go and see theatre regularly. In the US the situation has got far worse. On Broadway it is not inconceivable to pay as much as a hundred dollars for a seat. In the Soviet Union the average price is three roubles, approximately three pounds sterling or six dollars.

Work with the students continued to flourish. By this time the director Bill Gaskill, who was to continue the work after I left, had arrived, having suffered the usual initial chaos of hotels, etc. I had known Bill since my days at the Court, but I had never been directed by him. During those days in the late sixties when the Court was run by the triumvirate of Gaskill, Lindsay Anderson and Tony Page, the Court was polarised into two camps, the Anderson/Page camp and that of Gaskill and Peter Gill. Younger actors tended to work in one or other of these groups. I worked in the Anderson/Page camp. Like many of his generation who had worked at the Court, Bill's reputation as a director was mercurial. But his reputation as a teacher was second to none. In conversation during our time together in Moscow and Leningrad, I found him incredibly consistent in his views on the theatre. Examining Bill's career, one could see the journey of an artist who had spent his life struggling to maintain his beliefs against the worst aspects of shifting theatrical trends. As a fellow traveller it would be a great privilege for these young Russians to have the wealth of his insight and experience.

The trip to Leningrad had been arranged for the weekend. I seriously contemplated forgoing the journey as I felt it would be detrimental to break the flow of good work that I was now achieving with the students. Then I thought this might be the only chance I would ever get to see Leningrad. So on the Friday evening we took the overnight train, the Red Arrow, to the dream city of

Peter the Great. Leaving from Leningradsky Vokzal in Komsomol Square at 11.00 pm and arriving at the station in Nevsky Prospect at 8.00 am.

For the visitor a journey on a Soviet train is a must. In a land of astounding ataxia, the Soviet metro and train systems are the exception to the rule. The compartments are comfortable, the service exceptional: a cup of tea on retiring and a cup of tea on wakening.

Travelling through the night had an eerie effect. There was no darkness, only a winter twilight generated by the mounds of snow piled high at the side of the track. Our group consisted of Nadia, Richard, Hugh and Bill Gaskill. On arrival we were driven to the Leningrad Hotel and went through the usual tedium of checking in. Next to the Indians the Russians take the biscuit as far as bureaucratic nitpicking is concerned. The Leningrad Hotel was located on the Neva close to the Winter Palace. The rooms had a spectacular view of the river and where it splits into the Malaya (little) and the Bolshaya (large) Nevas. From my window, on the opposite shore I could see the cruiser, *Aurora*, whose guns had been turned on to the Winter Palace in 1917, signalling the start of the Revolution.

Leningrad, the jewel in the crown of Russian culture, the city of Dostoievski and Pushkin, where the genesis of contemporary Russian literature began. Built by Peter the Great on the marsh bogs of the Neva, the city is still comparatively young and, after the contrast of Moscow, overpoweringly European. As I gazed out at the ice breaking on the Neva, I felt humbled by the beauty of this unique creation of the Tsar. A monument to its founder. The blend of the cold Baltic light and the greys and yellow ochres of its pavements and buildings give the effect of a ghost rising out of the sea. A spectre of the past where the fires of the Revolution were kindled and where the ravages of war claimed more than six hundred and fifty thousand people dying of starvation and seventeen thousand murdered by the indiscriminate shelling of the invading German forces. For three years the siege was withstood and then Leningrad emerged from the gunsmoke as the cultural heartland of Russia.

In our whistle-stop forty-eight hours the doors of palace, theatre and museum were opened to us. The Hermitage with its long lines of Soviet families waiting to enjoy the Sunday splendour of revelling in the treasures of State and Tsar.

72

Bypassing the queue with the obligatory slip of paper, we made our way in through a side door, up some steps, past officialdom and into the museum to relish its delights. Suddenly for the first time since arriving in the Soviet Union, CHOICE. But what to choose from the treats that were held before us? Like a child in a toy store, who wishes to play with every toy in the shop, it was impossible to know where to begin. Never have I witnessed such a collection. It seemed that every painting ever painted was here in this building. In that brief hour I saw more Impressionist paintings than I had ever seen in the whole of my life, more Picassos than I'd seen in Western museums. The galleries were endless. They say that the basement of the Hermitage was at one point full of paintings and the staff were alarmed that dampness from the nearby Neva would irreparably damage these glorious works. As a preventive measure, it is said, these paintings were taken from the basement and stored in the flats and apartments of the workers of the museum. Personally, I couldn't imagine a more fitting way to see a Matisse than in the humble home of the gallery cleaner.

The main object of our visit was Leningrad's famous Gorki Theatre. We had been invited to attend a Sunday matinée of a musical directed by Georgi Tovstonogov. Based on a traditional story of the 1850s about a clerk who ends up becoming the boss, it was dismally disappointing. The music was trite and the production old-fashioned. The company were obviously very tired and jaded. I was reminded of my student days when I had sat enthralled at the breadth and range of their work. Now it was mechanical and soulless. Tovstonogov received us in his room, like the Pope or a potentate. He had become smug and was a little patronising. It was sad to see such a great theatre in this parlous state.

On the previous day, our host and one of the financial managers of the theatre, a charming roly-poly gentleman called Boris who had a tremendous knowledge of Dostoievski, took us to the apartment where the great man had lived in the last three years of his life. The size of the flat had a humbling effect. The image of a writer of such a tormented imagination living and working in close proximity to his family in a setting of domestic harmony was overwhelming. The room where he had his stroke, the couch he lay on, the simple household objects, created a vivid impression of normality. Later, I

73

was taken to the tenement where the original Raskolnikov slew the old woman in *Crime and Punishment*. Standing in the dark stairwell the whole story came to me afresh. Before visiting Russia and having been involved in productions of Russian plays or adaptations of novels, I imagined a largeness, a grandeur. I was surprised constantly by the mundane and prosaic nature of the source of these great plays and novels.

By contrast, at the Kirov, the home of Diaghilev, Nijinsky, Nureyev, Makarova and Baryshnikov, the sense of grandeur was positively engulfing. The stage alone seemed to go on for ever and the auditorium was vast. Unluckily we were unable to see a performance, but the building was like a homage to a time past.

It had been arranged that we should take tea that Saturday afternoon with a doyenne of the Leningrad acting corps, Alicia Freindlikh (pronounced *Friendly*). We decided to walk from the Kirov to Miss Friendly's apartment as we had a gap in our itinerary. On our way, we passed a small park still covered from the previous week's snow. Children of all shapes and sizes were making snowmen and playing on a solitary frozen slide. Grandmothers with prams, courting couples wrapped in their winter warmth. Idyllic. The park was in front of a beautiful blue building with white pillars. The Cathedral of Saint Nicholas, dedicated to the Russian navy, my first experience of a working Russian church. Welcomed by the church authorities, I watched as the worshippers went about their business. The expression on the faces was one of intense spiritual communion. The cathedral was on two levels, with two separate chapels, both brim-packed with either the very old or the very young. A memory of Leningrad and Moscow is of a preponderance of old people.

The solemnity and quiet of St Nicholas on that first visit was to be the antithesis of my second experience of Soviet church-going. In the wake of *perestroika* and coinciding with the celebration of a thousand years of the Orthodox religion, there was an air of hysterical religious fervour.

My last visit to Moscow was in the spring of 1988 and I arrived at *Paskha* (Russian Orthodox Easter), which is an especially holy time for the Soviet faithful. I was invited by the film actor, Oleg Yankovski, to attend a midnight mass at the Cathedral of the Old Believers in the city. The crowds surrounding the cathedral were practically of football-stadium proportions. I had never seen so many people at a religious service. The atmosphere was one of desperation, not celebration, the violence in the air was quite frightening. People were pushing and kicking one another aside to get a glimpse of the Patriarch's procession as the Host was carried through the church and outside around the perimeter of the building at midnight. Between the procession and the crowd were a phalanx of strong-armed ex-KGB types. Without these heavies I feared that the old ladies in the procession would have been crushed by the crowd. It was mayhem. One of the guards recognised Yankovski and allowed our group through to the front. As the gap opened to allow us through, there was a rush forward. I was the last to get through. Behind me, people were falling over. I was dismayed by the hysteria. The look on the faces was one of avaricious expectancy of something unobtainable. It left a profoundly uncomfortable feeling. What should have been an hour of pastoral reflection on the resurrection of Christ turned into an alarming nightmare. Yankovski told me later that in recent years the crowds at *Paskha* have quadrupled in size.

So, that Saturday afternoon in Leningrad, after leaving St Nicholas cathedral, we made our way towards the apartment of Alicia Freindlikh. Friendly by nature as well as by name, Alicia reminded me a little of the late Rachel Roberts. The vivacity of her personality and the contents of her samovar provided a welcoming warmth after our cold constitutional from St Nicholas. A star in her own right, Alicia Freindlikh had been with the Maly Theatre in Leningrad for a number of years, before recently making a move to join Tovstonogov's company at the Gorki Theatre. She spoke quite passable English. Her apartment was in one of the older nineteenth-century buildings with its wide, ornate staircases ascending six storeys. As in most of the buildings there was a great evidence of dilapidation. The apartment was quite spacious by Soviet standards, very much a dwelling of someone of high status within the Soviet system. Her husband was an artist, the flat, though dark and foreboding, hung with several paintings interspersed with the odd icon.

It was my first view of the home life of a Soviet artist. By Western standards, it was really quite modest, though in many ways reminiscent of an artist's apartment in New York. Her views on the theatre and her attitude to directors and writers were alarmingly similar to those held in the West. Hugh, who had been interviewing her, was impressed by her frankness. She very much resented the way the Russian theatre was moving towards a more fashionably conscious repertoire of work dealing with faddish social motifs which replaced genuine dramatic substance. An astute remark of hers quoted later by Hugh, 'When I play a writer like Dostoievski he holds me in the palm of his hand. When I act the work of some of these new writers I feel I'm carrying them on my back.'

She invited us to attend a benefit performance that evening at the Gorki Theatre of Neil Simon's *Last of the Red Hot Lovers*. Simon appeared to be cropping up wherever we went. It seemed a wholly inappropriate production to go to in Leningrad. The performance was a form of testimonial for an old actor who was celebrating his fifty years with the company and would be quite a unique event. The takings from the box office would be given to the old actor for his retirement. We succumbed.

I was amused by the idea of this testimonial. A common practice in England during the eighteenth and nineteenth centuries, actor's benefits had subsequently died out. I have often thought that it would be a good idea to revive this custom. Often, when I attend a memorial of some not so well known actor and note the turn-out of the congregation, I think how much better it would have been to honour the actor while they were still alive. A testimonial in a theatre on their behalf might have allowed them to have a bit of recognition and financial support in their old age.

During the performance we received a message to say that the dramaturge of the Maly would very much like to invite us to visit a rehearsal that Lev Dodin was conducting with the students from the Maly drama school. Having seen his superb work in Moscow, I was excited at the prospect of going to a rehearsal. We arrived at midnight in the middle of what seemed to be a dress rehearsal of a play about the Cossacks during the Revolution. We sat in the upstairs gallery in the small theatre. Periodically, a Russian voice would boom through the loudspeaker system into the auditorium. At first I thought that it was some mistake, perhaps a stage-door man giving pronouncements over the theatre tannoy wrongly connected during the performance. But no. After the voice, the young actors would make minor adjustments in their stage movements. We soon became aware that the voice was coming from below in the auditorium. This was Dodin directing his cast through a microphone at the back of the stalls. Gaskill and I were somewhat horrified at this technique employed at a dress rehearsal in such an impersonal and imperious fashion. I met Dodin later in London and he had been aware of our visit and was extremely shamefaced by his behaviour. Apparently the production had been quite fraught and the students found the work unfathomable. When we arrived they were way way behind in the schedule and, out of desperation, Dodin had resorted uncharacteristically to this draconian method. We all have our off-days.

Nine

Our time in Leningrad drew to a close. We caught the night train back to Moscow, arriving early in the morning. I went immediately to the MXAT school and continued rehearsing. As usual my students were on Moscow time, which meant that they were late. Timekeeping was not a generally observed ritual of Soviet life. In fairness the work schedule of the students was killing. School began for them at nine o'clock in the morning and they probably wouldn't see their dormitories until one or two o'clock the following morning. Many of them would be involved in performances at the MXAT as walk-ons. Some were already working for Tabakov in his studio as full-time actors. Some even were making films. How they could squeeze all of this into a day was quite beyond me, but they managed exceptionally well.

The life of a student in any society can be fairly rough. In the USSR it is positively sandpaper-coarse. The State provides them with forty roubles per month living allowance, a sterling equivalent of forty pounds. Out of this they have to feed and clothe themselves and pay a nominal rent. Usually they live in dormitories, fairly run-down buildings, sharing rooms with at least one other, sometimes two, sometimes even more. The one dormitory I visited had on each floor five box-like rooms, with two students apiece, a kitchen, one toilet and bathroom in the basement. All at the absolute basic. A few of these dormitories had many unwanted visitors that would appear in the middle of the night, rats.

Many of the students were married; the dormitories are segregated, separating husbands from wives. This quite naturally leads to sexual moonlighting after hours as a game of musical beds is played so that sweethearts can be reunited. The dormitory supervisors on the whole turn a blind eye, but some cruelly exercise their officious right. The students who live in these dormitories are in the main not native to Moscow. The Muscovite kids usually live with their families, though this creates problems as space to study is at a premium.

Rules concerning the movement of individuals between cities for employment have been quite strict. It is extremely difficult for a non-Muscovite, when leaving his educational institution, to get a job in Moscow. He or she is encouraged to return to the city or province of origin. As a result, there is a multifarious floating population in Moscow seeking to avoid this particular stricture. During my time at the school there were two such young men observing my class who had left the School Studio the previous year and had as yet been unable to secure positions in a theatre, mainly because the quota for non-Muscovites had been filled and these young men were without the necessary influence. Of course nepotism and favouritism goes quite a long way towards corrupting this particular aspect of the theatre and a star system clearly operates. It would possibly have been a benefit to these young men. But neither were favourites, nor did their fathers or uncles or cousins hold any particular position of Party power.

Eventually, the missing numbers turned up fresh from their weekend. This morning we would attempt *Macbeth*. Actually we had been attempting *Macbeth* for a few days. Unlike my forecast for *The Shrew*, this was proving the most difficult scene of all. The *Macbeth* scene begins with the famous dagger speech in which the Thane has a vision of a dagger that is directing his way towards the eventual murder of the King. Notoriously difficult. A landmine for the most experienced 'thesp'. The difficulty for student and actor is to plot the journey of the dagger in his head. In rehearsal I would use an actual physical dagger which would be held by one of the students and the student playing Macbeth would follow it with his eyes. I concentrated on doing the scene purely in dumb show before even beginning to look at the verse.

The question arose about supernatural experiences. In *Macbeth* the world of the supernatural has to be embraced. One has seen too many productions where this world becomes rationalised and grounded. Every one of us has had an experience which cannot be logically explained and it is necessary for the actor to use his emotional memory to rediscover that experience and translate it to the problems of the verse.

That morning I had gathered my three Macbeths and their ladies. This was the morning for ghost stories. It was interesting that these young Soviets appeared not to have had any psychic experiences. Or rather, if they'd had any they were unwilling to recount them. Perhaps out of embarrassment. Given that these were some of the most imaginative young men and women I had ever worked with, I found it surprising that they were so inhibited about the supernatural. I had to prise out of them any possible occurrences they may have had.

Talking about dreams and how they valued dreams in their waking life, we progressed towards the individual psychic experience. One of the group, Yuri Ekimov, an eccentric young man, related an incident that had happened to him when he first started as a student and was staying in one of the school dormitories. .

He was sharing the room with a fellow student and had come back one evening to find his bed occupied, he thought, by a drunken companion of his room mate. The two figures were asleep, so he slept on the chair at the end of his bed, tossing and turning, unable to find a position to relax. Suddenly he was woken by a light emanating from his bed. The bed started to rise and, terrified, he hid himself under his coat. In the morning he awoke, saw that the bed was still occupied, went and bathed. He returned to the room to find his friend awake.

He was extremely angry and said, 'How dare you give my bed to someone else.'

'What are you talking about?' said his room mate.

'My bed. This person who has been sleeping in it,' he replied.

'There's been nobody sleeping in your bed. You can see for yourself.'

Ekimov turned, looked at the bed. It was empty.

The students were rapt by his tale. Ekimov had cast a spell on the room. Of course, this story may have been all an elaborate fabrication on his part. But, true or false, what was important was that his power of imagination was exercised in a psychic form. And, like it or not, they had embraced collectively the notion of a supernatural experience. Now we could begin the dagger speech.

A major element of *Macbeth* is terror. Of course Ekimov's tale again serves as a lesson in terror. In the dagger scene it is necessary for the actor playing Lady Macbeth to maintain a balance between terror and action. The role poses many problems for the young actress. The received image of the part is of an evil, ambitious, greedy, pushy, domineering, castrating woman. All these elements have traces in the character, but they do not constitute the whole. She is a much more imaginatively drawn figure. The Macbeths are a duo, each compensating for the other's strengths and weaknesses. At the beginning of the dagger scene, Lady Macbeth is very much at the mercy of the murder taking place in Duncan's bedroom. Her first speech begins:

> That which hath made them drunk hath made me bold:
> What hath quench'd them hath given me fire.

These first two lines suggest someone who is very much in control of their own feelings, someone nerving themselves up for a big event. But then . . .

> . . . Hark! Peace!

She is disturbed. Her resolution is broken by the sound of an owl. And reassuring herself she continues:

> It was the owl that shriek'd, the fatal bellman,
> Which gives the stern'st good-night.

And again, nerving herself up. This time she runs through a check-list of her contribution to the evening's mayhem. Looking at the bedroom door where the murder of Duncan is taking place, she continues:

> . . . He is about it.
> The doors are open; and the surfeited grooms
> Do mock their charge with snores: I have drugg'd their
> possets,

> That Death and Nature do contend about them,
> Whether they live, or die.

We now know that she has drugged the guards of Duncan's bedroom. And obviously with a potion so strong that warrants the phrase, 'That Death and Nature do contend about them'. Suddenly, from offstage, Macbeth speaks:

> Who's there? What ho!

Now, why would he say this? The obvious answer is that he has heard her speaking and doesn't know who it is. For her, panic.

> Alack! I am afraid they have awak'd,
> And 'tis not done: – th'attempt and not the deed
> Confounds us.

The panic mounts and again she hears a sound from offstage.

> – Hark!

It's not my fault, she thinks to herself. She again consults her checklist.

> – I laid their daggers ready;
> He could not miss 'em.

She has made her contribution, hasn't she? She has done everything possible to prepare for the murder. She could have killed him herself?

> – Had he not resembled
> My father as he slept, I had done't.

Could she? It's extremely doubtful. Macbeth enters. She says,

> – My husband!

This last line proved an interesting point of debate about the translation. The version we used was Pasternak's, unquestionably the best translation of Shakespeare into Russian. He has translated this line as 'Macbet!' When the students played the scene in rehearsal, I, without consulting the text, always found this moment jarring. The path of Lady Macbeth's first speech graduates through a series of obstacles which she overcomes or rationalises. The path is signposted with a number of shocks, doubts, half-certainties, qualifications and self-justifications, finally emerging in need of reassurance. All underlined by a feeling of terror at what was going on in Duncan's bedroom.

Macbeth enters and in the Russian text she calls, 'Macbet', which is far too formal a greeting at this moment and in her present state. The actual sound of the word 'Macbet' (in translation the 'th' is substituted by the hard 't') has a hard, impersonal timbre. Of course, when I consulted the English text, the word was 'husband', which is much more personal and, because of the middle 's', has a softer sound and a much more reassuring tone when spoken aloud. We then went to the Russian for 'husband' and the Russian word is *muzh*, which again has a softer, more yielding sound when spoken aloud. The word *muzh* is synonymous with both husband and man. So, in fact, we would have the added bonus of her saying 'my man'.

Language is so much the formalisation of sounds – shaped and punctuated grunts and groans – which have powerful, primeval roots. The most basic are the sounds of warning and reassurance which all animals make. Dealing with babies who have no language, one communicates, apart from facial expression, by these sounds. Human speech is a formal and varied modulation of these two elements, interlaced with a third, the plaintive tone of desire, want. This third element is rooted in anguish. A domestic animal, wanting to be fed, can only make a generalised sound of anguish. The human baby, likewise, until he learns the vocabulary to describe his anguish. I believe that these three elements are the basis of all communication and that any given texts, Shakespeare, Chekhov, Beckett, etc. are musical and tonal variations of these elements, in differing degrees of sophistication. Having worked in three continents and in a variety of languages ranging from Russian to Bengali, Hindi to Japanese, in every instance an understanding of these three elements illuminated the indigenous culture.

The work on *Macbeth* continued. The scene still presented tremendous difficulties to my young band of Russian players. Obviously they needed to be liberated and have the burden of the scene lifted from their shoulders while still maintaining progress. One of the great obstacles for any actor is the intrusion of their ego. Ego of course has to be acknowledged, but in the end, it's a bloody nuisance. Sometimes, in being directed a young actor can feel his ego threatened. Things become disproportionate. There is too much at stake. They feel that they are being judged and their role becomes a burden; ego in the form of self-worth inhibits them. All the time they are looking over their shoulder, thinking, 'Does he like me? Am I being good? Will this lead to anything?' It is difficult in such situations to get the actor back on the rails of the rehearsal. A useful method is to set up an exercise to remove this burden by redistributing the weight of the part, i.e., make the actor share the part with another ego who is also looking over his or her shoulder.

So, we resorted to this sharing technique. Three Macbeths, three Lady Macbeths. All of which created a corporate personality, thereby illuminating for each individual player aspects of their performances that were lacking. They felt less scrutinised, less as if they were on trial. The pattern of work was easier for them to follow. What we used quite simply was a diversionary tactic, to direct the actor back to the work at hand. With our three ladies I would break the text between them so that they would share the lines, treat the experience as a game, dividing them into A, B and C and perhaps break up the text like this: 'A' would begin,

A: That which hath made them

And then 'B' would perhaps pick up,

B: . . . drunk

Then 'A' again,

A: . . . hath made me

84

And finally 'C' would say,

C: . . . bold.

Breaking up the text in this fashion gives each actress a marker towards understanding, first the use of the words in the speech and then her personal connection with those words. When actress 'B' says 'drunk' she has to examine within herself the notion of what the word implies for herself and then what it may imply for Lady Macbeth. Equally, actress 'C', when she says the word 'bold' has to make the same evaluation. And actress 'A' who has taken the considered position in the game with her line, 'That which hath made them . . .', and 'hath made me . . .' reflects upon the contemplative neutrality of these lines which act as a springboard for action.

With my young Russians I proceeded in this way, going even as far as having them play in musical unison with each other. The discipline that this required, instead of restricting them, as might be thought, actually had the opposite effect. They all began to feel the genesis of a separate identity, a responsibility towards steering the course of the scene and not being burdened by their characters.

I have always found the idea of character a ludicrous one. When actors say in the early stages of rehearsal 'my character wouldn't do that', I never understand what they mean. In life we have no notion of our character. We may know what we like and dislike. We may know what we are afraid of. But we never talk in terms of 'my character wouldn't do this'. The notion is ludicrous. As in life, so with the theatre. Also, the presupposition of 'my character' limits the mechanism for discovery. Closing doors which may lead to a greater potential than the actor at first thinks. The actor must keep himself open to all eventualities and not constrict himself by false notions of 'his or her character'. Perhaps after endless rehearsals and many many performances, they may have earned the right to refer to *their* character, but only then it seems to me.

The lessons I was learning about my own acting from these young Russians were inestimable: I began to see through them the value of total precision of thought and the need to create a greater harmony between voice and physical movement. Too often actors work on assumptions, the conceit of 'I think therefore I am', without the support of the necessary skills of voice and movement. And too often, as a result, our acting appears to happen in a dream-like state. The other lesson I learnt was the need not only to harmonise voice and movement, but also to centre my thoughts in relation to my actions. Often in performance actors push themselves too far and too quickly without allowing for the necessary centring of intellectual and instinctive powers. We are often guilty, because of the wish to achieve, of forcing the dramatic action. We push, embellish, and sacrifice simplicity for effect.

The balance between the states of thought and animation is a precarious one and the player must walk a careful tightrope in order to create the maximum effect with the minimum of effort.

Very gently, I began to wean the group away from the corporate Macbeth identity and back to their individual performances. The bonus was that any of the three Macbeths could play with any of the three Lady Ms. Each pair would be different and would illuminate the scene in a way that was unique to their permutation.

1a My mother, Molly.

1b My father, Chic.

2a Me aged 3.

2b Me aged 13 in Dundee.

3a With Fulton Mackay in 1969.

3b In Lindsay Anderson's production of David Storey's *In Celebration* at the Royal Court Theatre, London, 1975.

4a As Henry II with my son, Alan, in the BBC's thirteen-part drama, *The Devil's Crown*, written by Ken Taylor and Jack Russell, 1977.

4b Opposite Jane Lapotaire as Eleanor of Aquitaine, Henry II's wife.

5a As de Flores in Peter Gill's version of *The Changeling* at the Riverside Studios, Hammersmith, 1979.

5b Macbeth in the Cambridge Theatre Company's touring production in England and India, directed by Jonathan Lynn, 1980.

6a & **b** With Colum Convey
in *Rat in the Skull*
by Ron Hutchinson,
directed by
Max Stafford-Clark
at the Royal Court
Theatre, London, 1985.

7a As Paul Cash in Doug Lucie's *Fashion*, directed by Nick Hamm at The Other Place, Stratford-upon-Avon, 1987.

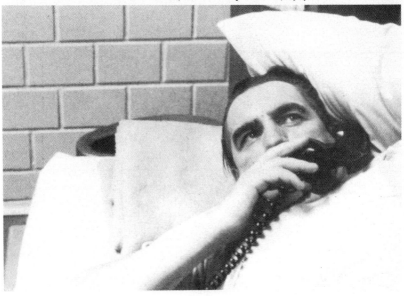

7b In the American film, *Manhunter*, directed by Michael Mann and co-starring William Petersen and Kim Greist, 1986/7.

8a As Titus in the RSC production of *Titus Andronicus*, directed by Deborah Warner, 1988.

8b As Vershinin, with Harriet Walter in the RSC production of *The Three Sisters*, directed by John Barton, 1988.

9 Outside the tenement building in Leningrad where the original Raskolnikov slew the old woman in Dostoievski's *Crime and Punishment*.

10a Rehearsing a scene from *The Taming of the Shrew*
with Irina Apeksimova at the Moscow Art Theatre School, 1988.

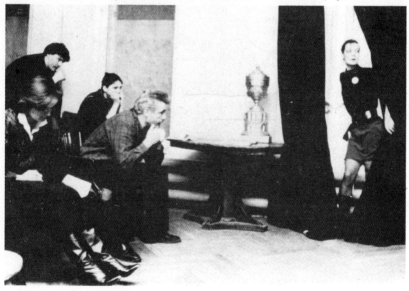

10b Rehearsing a scene from *Macbeth* with students
from the Moscow Art Theatre School.

11a In front of the Cathedral of Saint Nicholas, Leningrad.

11b In the Hermitage Square, Leningrad.

12 Students of the Moscow Art Theatre School. The line-up for
the Raising the Curtain gala at the Barbican Theatre, 25 September, 1988.
Back row (left to right): Valery V. Nikolaev, Yulia V. Menshova,
Sergei Kutzevalov, Ilia A. Voloch, Roman V. Kuzneschenko,
Mikhail Nemytchov, Igor P. Kozlov;
middle row: Sergei V. Shentalinski, Yuri A. Ekimov,
Marina D. Kolesnichenko, Vladimir L. Mashkov, Irina V. Apeksimova,
Ravyl A. Islianov;
front row: Lia N. Elsheveskaya, Tatiana G. Teslyar, Brian Cox,
Oleg Gerasimov (Dean of the Moscow Art Theatre School),
Nadezhda Y. Solovieva (Interpreter and Assistant to the Dean), Maria Kyedr.

Ten

With only three days to go till my departure for London, the students had reached a level of concentration whereby their grasp of the scenes was becoming surer and much stronger. A misconception among some of them had been that Shakespeare and Stanislavski were like oil and water and couldn't mix, that verse would not be open to the principles of Stanislavski's objective and super-objective approach. My job had been to show that verse structure was very much in line with objective and intention, i.e., the motivation of characters was contained in the way that verse and prose were threaded together throughout Shakespeare's writing. In poetic drama, whether it be Racine, Euripides or Shakespeare, there is a notion among students that verse distances grammatical speech, that the normal rules of grammar do not apply. But vital to a formative grasp of character and the movement of any dramatic action are the basics of language: subject, verb and object.

Once I had disestablished the gap between Shakespeare and Stanislavski, the pace of understanding and development quickened. The *Hamlet* scene was a perfect example of the fusion of two styles; the philosophic and intellectual nature of Hamlet's character plus Shakespeare's scene structure with its precise modulation of the verse. Probably the best example of the combination of verse and prose to work on. It begins with Hamlet's famous 'To be or not to be' soliloquy and ends with Ophelia's 'O what a noble mind is here o'erthrown'.

The great gift that the young Russian player has, because of a quality of weight crossed with volatile lightness and speed, is an unembarrassed combination of reflective and passionate prowess.

In the famous soliloquy, the Hamlet that Mashkov presented was that of a formidable intellectual, who in the scene with Ophelia

87

became a quixotic, highly emotional, dangerous young man. A truly heroic performance. Something which the contemporary British actor finds very difficult to achieve. The British tendency is to apologise, excuse those qualities which form Hamlet's personality – the intellectual and the poetic – and allow the neurotic to have the upper hand, because it appears to be the more interesting choice. In Hamlet neurosis is present, but only in part. He is an heroic voyager, a discoverer, a man with a burning quest. The young Russian has no problem with this. He understands well the poetic because poetry is a formidable part of the Russian, and subsequently the Soviet, culture. He understands the intellectual because the system of his schooling from day one is rooted in the power of knowledge and thought.

In acting terms the result is immediate.

When the soliloquy was spoken by Mashkov there was a disarming directness. I had the feeling that I was hearing this speech for the first time ever, because the argument was so pure.

At the end of the speech, Ophelia enters. The first four or five lines beween them are formal, respectful, yet distant, not the conversation of two people who know each other quite intimately. Shakespeare conducts the verse to a point where Hamlet breaks it, because the rhythm is betraying an unease in Ophelia's manner. The dialogue goes as follows:

HAMLET Soft you now. The fair Ophelia.
        Nymph in thy orisons be all my sins remembered.
OPHELIA Good my lord, how does your honour for this many a
                                                          day?
HAMLET I humbly thank you, well, well, well.
OPHELIA My lord, I have remembrances of yours
        That I have longed long to redeliver;
        I pray you now receive them.
HAMLET No, not, I never gave you aught.
OPHELIA My honour'd lord, I know right well you did,
        And with them words of so sweet breath composed
        As made the things more rich; their perfume lost.
        Take these again for to the noble mind,
        Rich gifts wax poor when givers prove unkind.
        There, my lord.

88

And at this point Hamlet breaks the rhythm of the iambic pentameter, electing to speak in prose. The effect on Ophelia is one of disorientation. As long as the verse structure was being observed in the manner of small talk she was safe and secure, but as soon as Hamlet breaks formality, her lines of communication become scrambled. He then starts throwing images, ideas, arguments about fidelity, womanhood, the procreation of the species and finally, accusing her of deceit. This is too much for this young girl who becomes a repository for his seemingly sick outpourings. At the end of the scene, she is left alone, and her only recourse to the verbal assault she has received is to resume the rhythm that had been broken. Over-emphatic in rhythm, presaging her mental deterioration with its insistent tone:

OPHELIA O what a noble mind is here o'erthrown!
          The courtier's, soldier's, scholar's eye, tongue, sword,
          Th'expectancy and rose of the fair State,
          The glass of fashion, and the mould of form,
          Th'observ'd of all observers, quite, quite down.
          And I of ladies most deject and wretched,
          That suck'd the honey of his music vows,
          Now see that noble, and most sovereign reason,
          Like sweet bells jangled out of tune, and harsh,
          That unmatch'd form a feature of blown youth,
          Blasted with ecstasy. O woe is me,
          T'have seen what I have seen: see what I see.

'Sweet bells jangled out of tune, and harsh.' Ophelia's speech brilliantly describes what we the audience have witnessed and is an indicator to the actors of the manner in which the scene should be played. It is amazing in Shakespeare how much of his stage directions are indicated in his dialogue. It is equally amazing how many directors and actors never seem aware of these directions.

For the young Russian actress, Alyona Khavanskaya, it was necessary to construct a pre-life to the scene à la Stanislavski. An image we used was of a young actress being pushed on to the stage, script in hand, to read a part in a play that she had neither seen nor read, working with an actor who will only improvise and not keep to the written text. So Claudius and Polonius were like director and stage manager, geeing her up, giving her Dutch courage and finally pushing her on to the stage. The effect was remarkable as she tried to hold on to her little bit of script and finally her sense of complete disorientation at Hamlet's refusal to stick to the lines written.

The level of work now being achieved was well beyond any expectations I had when preparations were being made for my trip. I had seen myself as an observer, not as a participator on such a scale. And I was uneasy about whether I would ever be able to come to terms with a language that was completely and totally alien. The line between bravery and foolhardiness is an extremely fine one.

I was lucky to be in Moscow at the bidding of someone who was even more foolhardy than I was, Tabakov. As protector and father of his group of young men and women at the MXAT Theatre School, it was evident that in this period of *perestroika*, he very much wanted these young men and women to be at the forefront of that movement towards openness, and by opening up channels of real active communication, of which Bill Gaskill and I had been beneficiaries, he would broaden the base of his school and the possibility to expand the brief of his fellow theatre practitioners in the USSR.

In 1986 he had been one of the prime movers in the organisation of a new actors' union, the Actors' Union of Russia. This was a body formed in opposition to the existing theatre union in order to break the stranglehold of bureaucracy that had previously existed. One of its main aims was to correct the anomalies that existed between the regional theatre and metropolitan theatres in the USSR, i.e. parity of wages, conditions, etc. To create better living and work conditions for actors and directors working in Soviet regional theatre. The other was to spread a net of international fellowship. Tabakov's main role was the development of international theatre relations. He had understood since his beginnings as a teacher the need to establish a context for the young actor that was much broader than the then existing communist ideology. This movement by theatre workers in the Soviet Union was very much a forerunner of *perestroika*.

On the penultimate day of my stay, Tabakov summoned me to his office for a final report on my progress with the students.

'They are simply the best students I have ever been privileged to work with. Their spiritual strength, professional conscientiousness and sense of identity is astonishing for people of their age. It has been an honour to have known them. I shall miss them when I go back to London,' I said.

'Then,' said Tabakov, 'you must return. I think it would be good if you were to work with them, perhaps just on one play.'

'It would be a wonderful idea,' I said. 'But my work schedule at the RSC would make it impossible. True, I do have the odd week or two when other productions are going on at the theatre. Maybe it would be possible, but very difficult . . .'

'We shall see,' said Tabakov.

I then asked him what should happen on the final day, for he was yet to see their work. I thought we would arrange a showing for him at the studio room we had been working in.

'I have a better idea,' he said. 'Maybe I invite some people and maybe we will go to the Actors' Club in Gorki Street to play these scenes.'

I hesitated, partly because I felt I did not want the kids to be unnecessarily exposed and partly because I felt what we were doing was not yet at the stage of playing to an audience.

'It's OK,' said Tabakov. 'It will be good for them to have a little exposure. Only a little.'

Reluctantly, I agreed. I was worried how conducive the space at the Actors' Club would be.

The Actors' Club in Gorki Street is a social centre for actors and workers in the theatre in Moscow. Schizophrenic in design, by day sedate, civilised, homely, a sort of proletarian Garrick Club. By night, rowdy, chaotic, grubby, reminiscent of the bygone days in London of the Buckstone, Jerry, or in extremis the Kismet clubs, actors' hostelries of the fifties and sixties. The building is spacious and uninspired in design, but with one or two good reception rooms for theatrical soirées. (Tragically, the Actors' Club burnt down in March 1990.)

The showing was to begin at eleven-thirty in the morning. I arrived at the club to be greeted by Hugh and Richard who had made their way from the nearby National Hotel.

'Quite a turnout,' said Hugh.

'What?' I said.

91

'For the showing. The room's packed. There's also a couple of television crews. One from Soviet television and one from ITN in London.'

'I don't believe you,' I said.

'See for yourself.'

He led me to a room on the first floor of the building. It was packed. There must have been as many as one hundred and fifty in the room. This was Tabakov's idea of a few people. My students by this time were arriving. They too were a little shocked by the reception, but extremely excited, with a great desire to rise to the challenge. 'Don't worry Brian. It will be all right,' said a voice at my shoulder. This was Masha.

From the very first day I had noticed a dark-haired, melancholic girl observing at the class. She had not missed one single session. On enquiring about her I discovered she was a design student in the first year at the school who had studied English and was now, apart from being a student, working for Tabakov as part-time secretary. Tabakov had three assistants in all at the school, all of whom, I later learnt, were studying English. Masha was atypical of a young Russian female student of her age: studious, enthusiastic and long-suffering. She became a useful liaison between myself and the acting students and this morning she had taken it upon herself to organise the prop requirements for the showing.

She greeted me that morning with a farewell bunch of roses and made a faltering speech of thanks for allowing her to attend the classes. I discovered later that she had stopped at every telephone kiosk in Gorki Street to check and double-check with her mother her English pronunciation. She joined Nadia in arranging what was needed for the performance in the room.

The students had assembled and were running through their lines, making their final preparations. And then, crisis. Somebody was missing. Angela, one of the Desdemonas; no one had seen her that morning. One had heard that her mother had been ill, another said that she herself had been ill. Her Othello was beside himself, perhaps she had gotten wind of this showing and decided it would be too much for her. I asked Yulia Menshova, who was playing the other Desdemona, if she would do the scene twice. She was only too delighted. Through Nadia, she said it would give her a chance to create yet another Desdemona.

Lastly, Tabakov arrived in great haste, eager to begin.

'Brian, after the showing you will please come to the small theatre we have here at the Actors' Club and maybe there will be some questions.'

'Who from?' I asked.

'Who knows?' he said.

I gestured to the room. 'I like your idea of a few people,' I said.

Tabakov smiled as if to say 'show business is show business'.

Finally the scenes began. All the supporters were keyed up with anticipation: Hugh and Richard, Masha and Nadia. As they launched into *The Taming of the Shrew* the palms of my hands became clammy and my heart started to pound faster and faster. Perhaps the whole thing was foolhardy, I thought. Just too ambitious? Maybe the kids had been over-keen in their enthusiasm? Perhaps I expected too much. After all, what had I really got to offer them? Just a few hackneyed ideas how to play the old Bill.

Soon, my pulse began to regulate and I became absorbed in the work. *The Shrew* was in full swing. As Petruchio, Shentalinski's lightness of playing and rooted fascination with Apeksimova's electric Katherine held the audience spellbound. Equally, Apeksimova's detailed shifts in attitude and her gamesome challenging of his masculine ego kept them in suspense. The double-edged laughter throughout the scene was a testament of their achievement and when she hit him, throughout the audience, you could feel a sense of danger. It was a total success.

This was followed by the three *Macbeth*s in rapid succession, each creating a different emphasis, challenging the audience's preconceptions of the scene. The *Othello*s with Menshova brilliantly contrasting the two Desdemonas; one, the rebellious father's daughter, the other, the unselfconscious flirt whose innocence seals her doom. Quite an astonishing *tour de force* by this young actress. Finally, the *Hamlet*. Mashkov showing the charismatic beginnings of a future Soviet star.

Then they were over.

There was a silence broken by the odd pair of hands clapping and one by one the whole audience joined in. Eventually, they were standing, applauding in that idiosyncratic Russian manner. The ovation went on for some minutes. The students seemed quite shocked, unsure of how they should respond. I was experiencing a whole mixture of emotions: relief, pride, gratitude, humility and a sense of disconnection from the event. What had taken place, it seemed to me in that moment, was something from which I was excluded. The way that each of these talented young men and women had risen to this occasion with such discipline, having at times been so undisciplined, left me quite agog at the breadth of their talent. For an instant they appeared quite consummate and unsurpassable and it had nothing to do with me and everything to do with them. It was a most odd feeling. Not being a woman I can't know, but I imagined it was like the severing of the umbilical cord.

Before I knew where I was, Tabakov was rushing me out of the room and into the hallway to talk to the Soviet TV crew. The students were also being interviewed by British ITN news. Within my earshot, I heard some of them speak in fluent English which, until that point, I had no idea they possessed. The youngest of our group, Tatiana Teslyar, a small dark, Moldavian girl with a bass voice, was speaking with an inspired fluency created by the heat of the moment.

Tabakov then ushered me into the main hall on the ground floor of the building. I was shocked to see that the place was packed with even more people than had been present at the showing of the students' work. These were practitioners not only from Moscow but from theatres thoughout the Soviet Union. With Tabakov in the chair, Bill Gaskill and I launched into a long question-and-answer session. It was as if we were emissaries from another planet, the eagerness and voraciousness with which the assembled crowd devoured our answers.

As my time in Moscow drew to its close, I felt a growing awareness that what I was witnessing was the birth of a new ideology, now confirmed by the hungry curiosity of the audience. Here before me was the wake-up call of Russian theatre culture and the possibility of my sharing in that awakening. Lying in my hotel bedroom I had felt an indefinable shadow hovering over me, a spectre, and in the months to come that spectre would take on a more and more palpable form.

94

After this session, I could not wait to rejoin those who had survived the flak of the morning shooting gallery. A small party was arranged in Tabakov's office. We Brits, leaving Bill Gaskill behind, were to catch our plane to London at five o'clock that afternoon. The farewells were, quite naturally, tearful. I had come closer to this group of young men and women than I had ever been to any in my life. The shadow of what they represented loomed large upon me. Presents were exchanged.

Finally, Tatiana, with her new-found fluency, said, 'You must come back. Soon.'

Eleven

It was Wednesday afternoon, 13 April 1988. I was lying on my back, on my living-room floor, reflecting on the trauma of reviving Doug Lucie's *Fashion* for the RSC. The play had just opened in London. Though a critical and box-office success, the production had been unravelling since its première at The Other Place, Stratford, the previous year. The general feeling among the cast was that a little re-writing and more specific direction would benefit the play immensely. It was hoped that both writer and director would be able to come together for the London production, but this had not been possible due to 'outstanding differences'. As usual, the production was held together by the actors, and throughout the year in Stratford we created a pretty formidable ensemble. We had been guaranteed that when *Fashion* came to London further work would be done, particularly to bring cohesion to the play's structure. But the author was unwilling to do this. He had lost faith in the ability of the director. And the director could not be withdrawn from the production due to contractual obligations with the RSC. Again the actors were left in the middle, it became a case of 'a plague on both your houses', and the show went on regardless. It was upsetting to witness Doug Lucie's tragic loss of faith in us. Lucie is a fine writer, he has something vital to say about the values by which we live and pursue our lives. There is no lonelier sight than that of a disenchanted writer in an actor's dressing-room on a first night.

As I pondered the events surrounding *Fashion*, the telephone rang. It was Carolyn Sands from BADA, she was very excited.

'They want you to go back.'

'Who?' I asked.

'The Russians.'

'When?'

'On Monday.'

'But that's crazy. It takes at least four weeks to get a . . .'

'You've got one. They will have a visa ready to be picked up by four o'clock tomorrow afternoon. Can you go?'

'For the visa?'

'No! To Russia! I'll arrange for the visa to be picked up. I've checked your repertoire schedule and you have no performances after Saturday for two weeks.'

'I know. I did tell Tabakov that I would return to Moscow if he wanted me to. Since I hadn't heard anything I assumed he didn't.'

'Can you go?'

'Well I suppose I can if . . .'

And that was that.

What to do?

I had intimated to Tabakov in Moscow that it would be interesting to work on a full production with the kids, but I had no idea that he would take me at my word and leave me with so little time for preparation.

I began to think furiously about a play that would be beneficial to the kids and give some point to my return journey. Because of what was happening politically and socially in the USSR, there was a great deal of political soul-searching going on in Moscow. A play had come to my mind during my last visit and I'd mentioned it to some of my students, but only in passing. The idea had come to me when I attended a performance of a new work at the Ermolava Theatre. I found the whole production very heavy-handed and quite unlike the quality of work I had come to expect. Produced by Valeri Fokin and performed by a fairly young company of actors, the play was a parable about the French Revolution with its all too obvious connections to 1917. The symbolism was unbelievably ponderous, the actors dressed in black PVC costumes, a combination of Soviet and French Revolution couture. Even so, there was obviously a great need within the young artists to examine their historic past and particularly at this point in their history. This was my clue.

What play in the English language deals so clearly with the ravages of a repressed society? Arthur Miller's *The Crucible*.

Dealing with the witch trials in Salem, Massachusetts, in 1692, when a group of pubescent young girls had turned tail on the puritanical community in which they were living and accused some of its members of witchcraft, the play was written as a scathing allegorical indictment of the McCarthy witch hunts of the late forties and early fifties, when prominent people in the United States were asked the question 'Are you now or have you ever been a member of the Communist Party?'

I suddenly became excited by the idea of turning the original intention of the play on its head and presenting it as an allegory of Russia's Stalinist past. In fact, the play merely had to be performed as it was written, the allegory and another intention would speak for itself.

A full production would be impossible as I had only two weeks to rehearse. Therefore I would probably only work on two or three acts. There was much to be done. Within five days I would be back in Moscow. I had no time to prepare.

I rang Carolyn Sands.

'Carolyn, can you call Moscow and tell them I will be working on Arthur Miller's *The Crucible*. Say that I would like to work with the same group that did the Shakespeare scenes. I will probably need at least twelve copies. Call me back when you have spoken to them.'

I went to my library and fished out a rather battered and well-worn copy of a play I hadn't read through since student days. To my horror I found that there were twenty speaking characters in the play. I'd been a little conservative in my estimate of copies. Obviously, there would have to be a lot of doubling of characters.

I began to read the play. As I finished, the telephone rang. It was Carolyn.

'I have spoken to Moscow. They're thrilled that you're coming and very excited about the idea of *The Crucible* and yes, they can get copies.'

I didn't tell Carolyn about underestimating the parts.

I put the phone down, and began to cast the play in my mind. The first decision I took was not to have any ageing in the play. The older roles would be played by students of great inner weight and intensity of character. I wanted the play to speak very much from the heart of these young people and not for them to be concerned with the externals of acting old people. Menshova, who was the most grounded actress of the group, would play Rebecca Nurse, and the giant Roman Kuzneschenko, whom I had not worked with on my previous visit, would play Giles Corey, the octogenarian farmer. Roman had a massive physical presence that young actors in the West simply did not possess. These two would be perfect for the elder characters. Mashkov would play John Proctor, Shentalinski, Hale and the crazy Ekimov, Parris. I had no Danforth in the group, so he would have to be cast from outside. Among the women Alyona would play Mary Warren, Tatiana Teslyar of the growly voice would play little Betty Parris and the beautiful Apeksimova, Abigail Williams. I decided to experiment and combine the characters of Mr and Mrs Putnam. The original Mrs Putnam in history was by all accounts a pretty formidable woman and I thought this would be perfect for Lia, who had acted a Lady Macbeth for me. The part of Elizabeth Proctor would be played by Marina Kolesnichenko, an actress of amazing spiritual intensity. Tituba, the black servant, was my only major headache. As far as I knew, there were no black actors in Moscow and the idea of a student blacking up was a particularly loathsome one. With the exception of this one major impediment, I felt I now had a cast for *The Crucible*.

A swift four days later, on Sunday, 17 April, I flew to Moscow. With thoughts of Salem still possessing me, I was met at the airport by Masha, Shentalinski and the indolent Nadia, with the customary bunch of flowers. This visit there was to be yet another new hotel, the Rossiya, a huge sixties edifice situated at the far end of Red Square, with a splendid view of St Basil's Cathedral. I drove to the hotel accompanied by my chaperons and rested for an hour.

At eight o'clock two of my other students woke me by phone to say that they were in front of the building. It was not possible for residents of Moscow to enter the larger tourist hotels – for fear of defection perhaps? How ludicrous. I stepped outside the hotel to find Ravyl and Menshova waiting for me in Moscow's cold night air. I hugged them both. Menshova could speak very good French, but little or no English. Ravyl, on the other hand, had an extraordinary grasp of English, completely self-taught. The son of a Tartar family, he had the most incredible self-motivation of any young man I have ever met. Not only had he taught himself English, but also the piano and the ability to read music. He was to be invaluable to me over the next two weeks as Nadia became less and less interested in the business of interpreting and more and more in the actual organisation of my itinerary.

We walked to the MXAT school through Red Square. It was exhilarating to be back in Moscow. When I got to the school, the whole group was there waiting, plus some eager to observe. They had bought, God knows how out of their meagre allowance, *champanskol*, Russian champagne. It was a very emotional reunion. Though it had only been four weeks since I last saw them, I had no guarantee that I would ever see them again, but here I was and here they were. They presented me with a samovar, an electric one! After much drinking and laughter, the whole bunch escorted me back to my hotel. I wanted to invite them all in, but an impossible doorman gave the ensemble black looks. I went to my room and settled down for the night whirling from both the speed of my return and the *champanskol*.

At nine o'clock the next morning I was greeted with a huge hug and beneficent grin by Tabakov in his office at the school.

'*The Crucible*? Yes, this play is good. We will do this play. You will work with the third-year students, yes? If you wish to include some others it is possible. Yes, this cast is good. OK. You will begin today. First you must cut the play, yes?'

'I have started already though I don't know how much of the play I should try to do in the time.'

'As much as you can. Maybe three acts.'

'Well, I can try.'

'You will do it. OK? OK. Brian, I must leave you now.'

'What about copies of the play?'

'They will arrive at two o'clock today. Yes? OK. If you need help, Gerasimov will see to your needs. I have to go to Helsinki for a few days.'

And the White Rabbit was gone again.

I continued to cut the text of the play, having started in England but finding it increasingly difficult. At noon I met four new students who agreed to play as cast. I had one copy of the play in Russian and two in English, my master copy and a copy for cutting. Nadia would translate the cuts from the cutting copy to the Russian text. Tituba, the black servant, had to go as it was impossible to find anyone who could interpret the part. It was a drastic step but I hoped that her offstage presence would permeate the action, still maintaining the tension of Act I. This proved particularly difficult in the last scene as Abigail had to incorporate some of Tituba's lines and Hale's exorcism at the end of Act I became doubly intense, but I felt at that stage it might just be possible to bring it off. With that decision I cut deeper into the play. Because of the cast availability I cut the part of Francis Nurse and Thomas Putnam as stated before, Giles Corey and Mrs Putnam incorporating both parts respectively. As I was cutting, the ghost of Arthur Miller rose before me. He would surely kill me I thought. I would if I was him. But I had only twelve days to create a reasonably coherent version of the work. So I cut deeper.

At two o'clock the phone rang. It was Masha to say that the scripts would now arrive at four-thirty.

I cut even deeper. (Sorry, Arthur, sorry, sorry!)

I was interrupted once again by one of the school bureaucrats, a homely lady of about forty-five who would arrange the timetable for my rehearsals. Apparently, I had been under the misapprehension that I had been working with one group on my previous visit, when, in fact, I had been working with students from the second and third years and I had cast from an amalgam of these two groups. These circumstances were extremely unusual, the point being the students had selected me just as much as I had selected them, so the timetable would have to be planned accordingly.

I received another call from Masha. The scripts would now *not* arrive until the next morning. I was beginning to feel under pressure as I had called for a reading of the play at six o'clock that evening, which would now not be possible unless . . .

At five forty-five in the evening I had finished transferring the cuts to the one Russian script that we had. At six o'clock the *The Crucible* cast arrived and we began reading the play, or rather Volodya Mashkov, who was playing Proctor, read the play as we still had only one copy. As the reading progressed, I cringed at the cuts. The atmosphere created by the reading was eerie. It was like being in a time warp with the young Anton Chekhov reading his new play to the gathered ensemble of the Moscow Art Theatre.

By eight-fifteen Mashkov had finished. The students were very excited. Great discussion followed. Their major worry was about the translation. They felt it was old-fashioned in form and too literary. I assured them that in the course of rehearsal we would endeavour to make the language more accessible both to them and ultimately to our audience. Nadia at this point intervened to remind me that the laws of copyright in the USSR were very strict and that I would have to be very careful in my handling of the text.

'It's all right, Nadia, I can just pretend that I didn't understand because of the language barrier.'

The students sniggered at this thought. The one heartening outcome was that they did feel the play had enormous relevance to their collective past and each individual's connection to that past. So my day ended happily. I went to my bed relieved that tomorrow we could immediately start to work.

I arrived promptly for rehearsal the following morning. And I sat and waited. After forty-five minutes I still had no students. As on my previous visit to Moscow, torrential turbulence seemed to be the order of the day before it settled into stormy chaos. Nadia informed me that the timetable was in tumult, classes had been disrupted. 'Political Economy' was the priority of the hour. Political Economy? Apparently, due to an unawareness of my agreed rehearsal times and a misunderstanding in translation, Gerasimov, Tabakov's deputy, had sent the majority of my class to attend their compulsory three-hour indoctrination class in Lenin, Marx, Engels and the other lads.

At eleven-thirty I had some students, but still no bloody scripts.

Impotence had superseded Political Economy. Volodya, who might play John Proctor – if I ever got round to doing the wretched play – began to recite an improvised stanza on the hazards of Soviet bureaucratic life. The splendid Shentalinski, who was the 'uncle' of the group, decided to take the law into his own hands and reorganise the timetable. After some minutes, Tabakov appeared from nowhere. I was under the misapprehension that he was off in Helsinki. Not so. He apologised for any misunderstanding. Apparently, the homely lady in charge of the timetable had boobed, Political Economy classes are a delicate matter. The professor in charge is always complaining about students cutting his class. Tabakov jokingly declared that he would be accused of being an anglophile imperialist. A volume of Russian verbiage ricocheted around the room between master and student; interpreter and interpretee. Again, I was struck by the preposterous notion of a Revolution in Russia and that, as it did happen, life must indeed have been really, *really* bad!

I sat at the end of the long table in Tabakov's office like an uncomprehending infant at a childminder's, bemused by the language flying thick and fast around my head. Sometimes a feeling of total incomprehension could have a comforting effect, like being wrapped in a huge Russian blanket. The telephone rang again. Tabakov answered. He looked at me and informed me that the scripts would not now arrive until three o'clock. The blanket dropped and I sat naked, cold and shivering with anger.

By two o'clock Tabakov indeed had gone to Finland. This was the time he was always leaving apparently, a misunderstanding based on his broken English and my non-existent Russian and of course we still had . . . *no fucking scripts*!

Before he left, he came clean about the real reason for the lack of scripts. There are no privately owned Xerox machines in Moscow. Ones were available to non-Russians, but not for Soviet citizens. Our scripts were stalled in a queue at some official Xerox department or other. Tabakov had bribed a minion at the Xerox plant for us to jump the queue. But at the last moment, a huge batch of documents from another organisation, higher in status than the Moscow Art Theatre, had to be copied before us. So we had lost our place in the queue. I had a rehearsal planned for six-thirty that evening which would be scriptless unless an act of God intervened.

Suddenly, there was another outbreak of loquacious Russian. Two of my new actresses had decided that they didn't like their parts and no longer wanted to be in the play. Masha shamefacedly left the room. Nadia exuded an air of weary resignation. The other students had embarrassedly avoided my eye. Nobody wanted to tell me the bad news, after everything else that had happened, in case it would have upset me. By that point, anger had turned to boiling rage. I thought that my brain would explode. To the rescue came Lia and Yulia. They said they would be delighted to double the parts of the two young servant girls.

If I didn't get any scripts by six-thirty, it would be impossible to continue with the project as I was already two days behind and had only eleven days left. I just didn't know how I could manage to pull it off. The students by now were as frustrated and angry as me that greater preparation had not been made by the staff of the school. I suspect that Tabakov had given no warning to the school and, anyway, he had gone. I continued to pray for a miracle.

At six-thirty my prayers were answered. A miracle had happened in the person of Masha. From three o'clock in the afternoon, she had mustered the troops of the school typing pool and with three typists, using the old-fashioned carbon-ribbon method, had succeeded in producing ten copies of Act I. She would work into the night to get the second act and on the morrow she would start Act III.

At 6.40 pm, against all odds, we started to rehearse *The Crucible*. Salem had arrived in Moscow.

Twelve

The first act of *The Crucible* takes place in the upper bedroom of the Reverend Parris's house in Salem, Massachusetts. His daughter, Betty, lies in bed inert, in a state of self-induced trauma. The previous night he had surprised a group of girls dancing in the forest, among them were Betty, Tituba his servant and Abigail Williams his niece and ring-leader of the group. Parris kneels by the bed distractedly praying.

At this early stage of rehearsal it was very important to establish the Reverend Parris's credentials in the play. The pitfall of the part is that he can be seen as either villain or comic relief. I knew that I had taken a risk casting Ekimov because of his tendency towards waywardness in performance. The Reverend Parris's role is crucial in the dramatic unfolding of *The Crucible*. Ekimov had a quality of obsession which was accurate for the role, but he also required an understanding of Parris's political position and his desire to keep his spiritual community together.

At the beginning of the play, because of the events of the previous night, Parris realises instantly that he is fighting to maintain his spiritual status with his Salem parishioners. The fight is real and has to be seen to be such. If the actor playing the role in any way patronises the character he will undermine the argument of the play. Straight away I realised that Ekimov must be steered towards a total understanding of his character's point of view. This would prove to be a major struggle throughout the whole of the production of *The Crucible*.

The brilliance of Miller's writing lies partly in his ability to show how the most intimate aspects of personal desire reflect man's position in the forming of communal doctrines and his responsibility for preserving those doctrines. If the doctrines are evil, man is usually motivated by vested interests to preserve his stake. Deputy Governor Danforth's desire for the preservation of the theocratic constitution of Massachusetts is an example of this. The witch trials coincided with a period of great social upheaval within the state. Danforth's need to make the witches of Salem a scapegoat was in order to set an example to the whole state of Massachusetts. Also, quite cynically, his status as Deputy Governor would be threatened by failure to root out the 'evil' in Salem.

In *The Crucible* Miller debates the constituent qualities of good and evil and how they apply to the people of Salem. In his writings about the play Miller clearly applies this to his central protagonist, John Proctor. But equally, and I am sure he would agree, this premise has to be applied in the preparation of the performance of the antagonistic characters, Parris, the Putnams, Danforth and even the small part of Cheever, the arresting officer in the second act. Of course, Proctor's relationship with Abigail is what causes the tiny tear, which grows to be a prodigious rip, in the fabric of Salem's society.

Act I concentrates on the first rending. Betty lying in bed. It is almost as if she is dreaming the events. Parris's panic, the growing terror of the serving girls and Tituba, Proctor's still-present lust for Abigail, the rival factions of the Putnam, Nurse and Corey families, the superstition of the village elders, the first murmurings of witchcraft and finally the presence of the witchfinder, Hale, his cross-examination of Tituba and Abigail. All happening in one little girl's bedroom.

After the delays of the previous two days, at that first rehearsal the colours were nailed firmly to the mast. Ekimov was clearly apprised of the task ahead of him.

The rehearsals moved at an exhilarating pace over the next ten days. I worked from nine o'clock in the morning to sometimes one o'clock the following morning with a movable break of about two hours during the day. I barely saw daylight. The only theatre visited was at the MXAT, usually when my students were themselves engaged in performances. The theatre being so close, I would pop in to see an act or two. The company had now returned from Japan and were beginning work on a new season of work.

My one social outing was to the flat of Oleg Borisov to have dinner with him and his wife, Efremov and Anastasia Vertinskaya. They were full of tales about their trip to Japan and had bought televisions and stereo systems paid out of their Japanese earnings. These had been shipped in container wagons to Vladivostok and brought overland by train. The hysteria of the evening was induced by the fact that Vertinskaya had bought a refrigerator. Her flat had been renovated in order to make space for it. Once installed, however, it was found to be inoperable. A vital spare part would have to come from Japan. This anticlimax caused a great deal of mirth among the group. Efremov then recounted a story of how when Tovstonogov's Leningrad company toured South America, he'd decided it would be cheaper if the sets were stored under tarpaulins on the deck of the ship. There was a storm in the Bay of Biscay and all the scenery for three of their major productions was swept overboard.

Efremov had taken over the running of the MXAT Theatre in the mid-seventies. The company had received particularly bad notices on its London appearances as part of Peter Daubeny's World Theatre Season in the 1970s. Most British critics thought the productions poor and the company well past its prime, a pale reflection of its legendary self, particularly in playing Chekhov's *The Seagull*. The shock waves of this reverberated back in Moscow and the powers that be decided that it was time for a change at the MXAT, so Efremov was brought in to revitalise the company. Later, he was joined by Tatiana Doronina from the Mayakovski Theatre. By the early eighties Efremov felt that the company had over-expanded with as many as sixty plays in its repertoire, some of which had been in production for over forty years. By that point the MXAT had moved into a new building on Pushkinski Boulevard. Unhappy with the loss of intimacy in the playing and seating space, Efremov felt there was far too great a separation between the members of the audience and longed for the days of the comfortable old MXAT in the Art Theatre Passage just off Gorki Street where the audience would sit elbow-to-elbow and actually make intimate contact with one another.

The old MXAT, an art deco building, built under the direction of Nemirovich-Danchenko and Stanislavski themselves, had fallen into disrepair and was in the process of urgent renovation. In 1984 the company was split in two, so, effectively, there were now two Moscow Art Theatres: one in Stanislavski's original building under the artistic direction of Efremov and the other, in Pushkinski Boulevard under the artistic direction of Doronina. It reminded me of Chekhov's line in *The Three Sisters* when Solyony says 'There are two universities in Moscow, the old and the new.' Now, there are two MXATs. I first learnt this when the taxi from my hotel habitually took me to the wrong theatre.

By the end of the first week I had succeeded in working Act I and half of Act II of *The Crucible*. Act I presented the most difficult staging problems because of the lack of space. It was set in a child's bedroom and in the course of the act there were as many as eight people on stage. I was continually reminded of the boiled-eggs sketch in the Marx Brothers film *A Night at the Opera*. They're on board ship and their cabin increasingly fills with people, giving no one room to breathe. It wasn't difficult to justify people visiting the bedroom to have a view of the child. It was only impossible to justify them staying there for the length of the act. In the end it was a question of making necessity a virtue and emphasising the lack of space and scale of these grown-ups in relationship to the child in bed. My worst headache was when the actor playing Giles Corey, Roman Kuznes-chenko, came into the room and suddenly there was a loss of light as well as space. Roman is six foot six inches tall and broad to boot.

These staging problems were solvable. But what was increasingly unsolvable was the absence of a Tituba. I had tried to make her a presence offstage, but after a while, it became clear to me that as every single character, apart from Danforth and Elizabeth, appeared in the scene, it was nonsensical that Tituba did not. At the end of the first act, I made Abigail the total object of Hale's onslaught when he is nosing out the witchcraft. The actors liked this compromise, but to me it was plainly silly. Perhaps a day or two away from the scene would provide a new perspective.

Act II was progressing well and it was clear that Miller's hypothesis of the play was contained in this act.

The setting is the Proctors' farmhouse at sunset. The witchcraft trials have already begun in Salem. Elizabeth Proctor prepares supper for her husband, John, who has been working in the fields. Their servant, Mary Warren, is one of the chief prosecution witnesses at the trial. She returns during the act and tells them that Elizabeth has been implicated in the trials by Abigail Williams. The Reverend Hale arrives and questions them about the Christian state of their household. As the act progresses news is received of the arrest of prominent members of the community, Rebecca Nurse and Martha Corey.

The sense of domesticity generated by Mashkov and Marina Kolesnichenko was excellent, but it was necessary to elaborate also the sexual side of their relationship. In reading historical accounts of the original Salem trials it's quite clear that most of the girls involved were in a pubescent state, their awareness of sex and sexuality at its most acute. Many accusations of witchcraft involved people claiming night-time visits to their bed by spectres. Elizabeth's coolness towards Proctor comes from the fact that she knows he has slept with Abigail Williams. Proctor's guilt of sexual infidelity is the root of the girls' hysteria, which will soon express itself in the multiple accusations of witchcraft. Proctor's desire is to reunite himself not only domestically, but sexually, with Elizabeth, to rekindle the fire of their love. It is also the very reason why this play is hot and passionate, not cold and detached. The smouldering triangle of Abigail, Elizabeth and Proctor erupts into flames that consume the whole community.

Shentalinski, as the witch-hunter Hale, struck the right note of optimistic relish in the first act. Miller describes him as an 'eager-eyed intellectual' and Shentalinski's position in the group as a solver of problems was very much mirrored in his performance as Hale. In the second act, Hale is somewhat chastened by the growing number of accused at the trials. Shentalinski's difficulty was to marry the optimism of the first act with the intellectual probity of the second. Again, the danger in playing a character like Hale is to patronise him, to treat him as a well-meaning buffoon. It is my belief that elements of this buffoonery must be present, but then transformed into a spiritual joy. Hale firmly believes in the validity of his spiritual position as an exorcist of evil, and he clearly revels in his use of the various books of learning that he brings with him in the first act like the young visiting MD eager to cure the world with his new-found healing power. The line that Shentalinski had to follow was the fine one between comedy and tragedy. By the end of the play, Hale emerges as a man tortured on the rack of his own blind faith.

Alyona Khavanskaya was making progress as Mary Warren, emphasising Mary's loneliness and her desire to be part of the group. Abigail clearly dominates her, but doesn't understand Mary's real need to be the centre of attention. Nowhere is this clearer than in the second act when she returns from the trial having been the star witness and behaves a little prima donna-ish. Alyona was very quick to take this line, but distrustful of Mary's sudden loquaciousness. We devised the notion of drinking from the bottle of cider which Proctor had previously used in the scene. This was a prop she needed to loosen her tongue. I hoped in time that I would be able to wean her away from this and allow her new-found garrulous personality to emerge as a consequence of her status as star witness at the trial.

On the Monday morning of the second week I received the news that the actor who had been cast as Danforth no longer wanted to play the role. He felt it was beneath his talents. By then I had thought I was beginning to see the light at the end of the tunnel.

I think quite a few of the actors had a natural suspicion of working with anyone who couldn't communicate in their language. The trust required by either side during a production must be absolute. None of these students had been in any way obliged by the school authorities to take part in either my earlier Shakespeare classes or the current work on *The Crucible*. The school staff very clearly regarded my presence as experimental and I was in no position to argue if a student dropped out. Perhaps I was being a little over-sensitive, but I took this withdrawal as a grave personal setback. I consulted the group to see if they had any ideas as to who might take over.

That lunchtime Irina Apeksimova came to me and suggested a fellow third-year student who would like to take over the part of Danforth. I was desperate and in no position to be fussy. She introduced the young man to me, Valery Nikolaev. I remembered him as the boy who, on my previous visit, had played an offstage Baptista in *The Taming of the Shrew*. As an exercise I had wanted Katherine to be forcibly pushed on stage by her father Baptista and

Valery happened to be in the vicinity when we were rehearsing the scene. He didn't bear the slightest resemblance to the character of Danforth. Danforth is described as a grave man in his sixties, sophisticated and patrician. This boy must have been in his early twenties, dark, balletic and a little droll. The idea seemed preposterous. No one would believe in him as a Deputy Governor. And then suddenly I was struck by the thought of the Kennedys, themselves natives of Massachusetts, young men who had risen very fast in their political careers and, in particular, Robert Kennedy, who at thirty-three had been the youngest Attorney-General in US history. He would provide a perfect role model. Suddenly a new interpretation of Danforth came into focus. A young man on the brink of a brilliant political career who would make enormous capital out of such a trial in Salem. A political *enfant terrible*.

Without more ado, I informed Nikolaev that he had the part. He was shocked. I told him that it might be a risk but, as far as I was concerned, a risk worth taking. We agreed he would come to rehearsal the following morning.

Nikolaev's approach at his first rehearsal was admirable. With great skill and rigour he began to build the foundations of Danforth's personality. His style was quite unlike what I had been used to from his Soviet compatriots. It was almost American: restrained, understated and analytically detailed. He was equally matched by Igor Kozlov's Hawthorne. Hawthorne's part is not huge in dialogue, but his effect as a watchful and silent figure of the establishment is acute throughout the third act. Kozlov's demeanour was that of a vigilant tiger sizing up its prey and never once, during the entire rehearsals of *The Crucible*, did his concentration waver.

The next three days were spent in detailed attention to the third act. Act III takes place in a vestry room at the Salem meeting-house. Offstage the trials are in full swing. In terms of staging, this part could not be more different from the first act. The possibilities are enormous. The setting being publicly formal and then, as the scene progresses into the cross-examination of the girls, becoming more and more fractured and finally, the debacle of Proctor and Hale's renunciation of the trial. It is brilliantly theatrical, but needs careful choreography and delicate control.

For the first time I felt the cuts that I imposed made sense. By removing Francis Nurse and combining him with Giles Corey, the benefits paid off, particularly in this act. The dramatic conflict tightened. The depositions presented to Danforth had the effect of focusing the action rather than dissipating it. At each rehearsal Nikolaev grew in confidence. The foursome of Danforth, Hale, Parris and Hawthorne, representing the oppressive Puritan establishment of Massachusetts, played together and off each other like a masterful string quartet, each complementing and balancing the other's nuance and tone.

Halfway through the second day came the entrance of the bewitched girls. Their foursome counterpointed the quartet of the establishment. The main acting difficulty for the four was how to create the growing crescendo of hysteria that is crucial in the closing stages of the act. We examined several behavioural parallels that might help them in the scene, like the pressure young girls at school impose within their own peer group to turn on any girl who breaks step. We also likened their behaviour to the savagery of animal packs when they turn and terrorise the weakest member who cannot keep up in their play. I reminded the girls of the cruelty in the scene and how they were no longer individual, but like bonded marauding animals they were hungry for prey.

Every pack has a leader and in this instance Abigail stands out as the girls abdicate responsibility to her. Abigail thrives on the power she has been given. She exercises it in the vivid use of her imagination. She becomes reckless and daring, even going so far as to caution Deputy Governor Danforth that he himself is not exempt from the power of the devil. Abigail, like a young diva, reaches the pinnacle of her performing career.

Apeksimova's grasp of the part was total. Her only problem was in deciding how conscious or unconscious Abigail was in her motivations. She struggled with this until the opening performance. A tendency the young actor has to be made aware of and avoid is to judge the person they are playing. By judging we minimise the incentive of the individual's inner reality. We can so easily fall into the trap of creating a cipher and evade discovering the genuine source of human motivation.

I knew that once the groundwork of Act III had been firmly

established for Apeksimova and the girls, they would be fearless in allowing the hysteria to reach its fever pitch.

Lying in my hotel room at night as the final rehearsals for *The Crucible* were being concluded, I was enveloped by a curious sense of *déjà vu*. The spectre that had overwhelmed me at the end of my last visit once again took possession of me. But it had turned friendly. What I had been given during these journeys was a tremendous gift, an insight into the workings of a culture alien to my own. A culture that was not afraid to take itself passionately seriously. I had come to teach, but in the tradition of Michael Gough, my first actor-teacher when I was a student, I had learnt far more than I was ever able to teach. On this trip, I was discovering a new pride in my work, or rather a hint of where my work could lead.

These young Russians had pushed me into rediscovering the nexus of my life in art. To put it simply, they had restored my faith in the power of theatre, in the power of *my* working in the theatre. I now felt the need to repay them in some way. But how? The gift they had given me had been themselves and I wanted to share myself with them in return. Suddenly I thought how exciting it would be if I could take them back to England and inspire others there as I had been inspired here. Then I thought, why not? Might it not also be possible to bring a group of young British actors to Moscow so they could study Chekhov and Ostrovsky? I thought about my teaching over the last twenty years, remembering my first group at LAMDA, the young Americans at Oxford and BADA, students I had worked with in India and the young actors whose enthusiasm had formed the backbone of the company at the RSC. In the spirit of *glasnost* (openness) I thought how these young Russian men and women could be the vanguard for a whole movement of international exchange. Exchange of teachers like myself was too limited, too partial. But an ensemble of young men and women, Russian and British, at the most impressionable and formative stage of their lives, would put the emphasis where it belonged: on a student body, not on its faculty.

I remembered the preconceived notions I had before I embarked on this Russian odyssey. I realised that throughout my life Cold War myths of Russia had gripped me as tightly as the prejudices exposed in Miller's *The Crucible*; myths compounded by the media which no one in British society could easily escape. I had succumbed to these conditioning influences. I thought that the same must be true in the Soviet Union, each of us blindly reassured in our ignorance and stereotyping of one another: the bowler-hatted Londoner in his pin-striped suit, the sable-hatted Muscovite in his standard KGB overcoat. The driving purpose behind such an exchange of student bodies through the arts would be to somehow dispel these received ideas. Indeed there were ingrained differences between cultures but no one seemed prepared to ferret out, recognise and celebrate the similarities. Through art-training exchanges – drama, music, opera, ballet, painting, sculpture – perhaps a common bond could be forged which would warm up peace after a long Cold War.

Being in Moscow, I had learnt as much about myself as I had about these young men and women. I was emphatic in my wish to share this experience in a much bigger way; to quote La Rochefoucauld: 'Nation to nation, country to country, people to people.'

Thirteen

I could hardly contain my excitement. As soon as I arrived at the school the following morning I buttonholed Tabakov.

'I want to invite the students to London.' (At this point I was perfectly prepared to put them up in my flat.)

I then told him my plans for the exchange. I asked if it would be possible for me to call London. Tabakov was intrigued by the idea. During the break in the afternoon, I called London and spoke to Tony Branch at BADA.

'Tony, I want to bring these students back to England. I'd like to run a course for them, a more comprehensive study of Shakespeare. With a bit of luck I could possibly get some assistance from the RSC. How do you feel about being their sponsors?'

Tony thought for a minute and then said, 'Why not?' and after a moment, 'When would you want them to come?'

'Probably September,' I said, working out my RSC timetable in my head.

Tony said, 'I'll see what I can do.'

Throughout that morning, Tabakov had been mulling over the idea of the exchange. He summoned me to his office later that afternoon.

'I think perhaps, Brian, we will do *The Crucible* as our diploma production. Can you return to Moscow?'

'Perfect,' I said. 'That would be wonderful. I have a gap at the end of September in my repertoire at the RSC. If the students come at the beginning of September for the Shakespeare course, I could continue rehearsals for *The Crucible* in London.'

'Fine,' he said. 'Now, you will need a designer for this production because the sets have to be made in July if we hope to open in the

MXAT Theatre Studio in September. I have a very good designer in mind, Sergei Kutzevalov . . .'

Then the weight of it all hit me. During my excitement about the exchange, I hadn't realised what I was committing myself to.

'You mean I would direct a production here?' not sure if I had heard correctly.

'Yes,' said Tabakov.

'In the Moscow Art Theatre?'

'Yes,' he affirmed.

'In the building where the plays of Chekhov, Bulgakov, Gorki, were first performed?'

'Yes,' said Tabakov. 'It's not inconceivable.'

I was completely gobsmacked. I couldn't quite take it in. I would actually direct a production at the Moscow Art Theatre. Students, yes, but at the Moscow Art. Jesus!

I would leave Moscow on the Sunday afternoon. It was now Friday morning. The designer and I were to meet later that day to discuss the sets. I had already decided that Masha, who had been such a help to me, might submit designs for the costumes. Nadia was over the moon with excitement about the possibility of coming to England. She had been hinting at such a possibility throughout my entire trip and now it had become a reality. She was formulating plans.

It was necessary to draw up a list of all who were to be invited to England. Tabakov wanted to see a run of the play before I left on Sunday. I gathered the cast together and told them he would be coming. They were delighted. As there were only two days left it was important not to break their concentration, so I decided not to tell them about the trip to England until after the run-through on Sunday afternoon.

Kutzevalov, the designer, arrived and we discussed the sets. I had already visualised the production, almost from the first day of rehearsal. I had created an outline for the actors to work in and emphasised to Kutzevalov that he must take this outline as the basis of his design. At the moment, only three acts had been worked on. It was my intention to finish the fourth act when they came to London.

There was only a little over a day and a half to rehearse till we presented the work we had achieved so far. Acts II and III were still rough but in surprisingly good shape. Nevertheless, the raw energy present in both these middle acts was still lacking in the first. Individual scenes were playing well, but there was still a lack of cohesion throughout the whole opening act. It was plagued by the absence of a Tituba.

The last seventy-two hours had been unbelievably smooth. I should have known that it wouldn't last. At the end of rehearsal late on the Friday evening, I was working out the call for nine o'clock the following morning, which would be my last full day of work. Suddenly there was general consternation among the cast. I asked Nadia what was wrong. She turned to me with her usual long-suffering look.

'Well, Brian, apparently . . .' she began in her indolent tone. 'Apparently there is a dress rehearsal tomorrow of a play at Tabakov's Studio.'

'So?' I said. 'They can't go. They'll have to see it some other time.'

'But you don't understand,' she continued, 'they are performing.'

'What?' I said. 'Why wasn't I informed?'

'I don't know,' she said. 'I think someone must have forgotten to tell you.'

'*Forgotten???*' Having hitherto restrained my language, at this point I let fly with a few well-chosen expletives which transcended any language barrier. Everybody was amazed. My outbreak lasted for some minutes. They just stared at me in benign amusement.

I would now not be able to rehearse with them on Saturday morning. So, I thought, 'If you can't beat them, you better join them.' This would be my last theatre outing before I returned to London.

Alexander Galin had been a writer who had spent a great deal of time working in the provincial theatre in Russia. His play, *Stars in the Morning Sky*, about prostitution in Moscow during the time of the Moscow Olympics, had been a runaway success when it premièred at the Maly Theatre in Leningrad. He'd re-established himself as one of the best playwrights in the Soviet Union. Previously he'd directed a number of productions but never his own work. On the strength of the success of the play at the Maly, Tabakov invited him to his Studio to direct his satire, *Dyra (The Hole)*. This was the dress rehearsal with half my cast in it that I attended that Saturday morning.

The final rehearsal of a new play in Moscow is an occasion of great buzz and speculation. That morning was no exception. The satire was based on a misunderstanding. The Hole is a small backwater somewhere in the USSR. The local bureaucrats have received a telegram from Party HQ saying that they have to prepare two hundred barrels of salt. The telegram is signed by the Party chief whose name is Sparrow. The officious bureaucrats misread the telegram as 'Please prepare two hundred barrels of salted sparrows'. The thread of the plot hangs on this misunderstanding. The production was brilliantly funny, using the stage to its maximum potential it involved dance, music, singing, knockabout farce and bathos.

I was enjoying myself enormously and in the middle of the first act, I turned to Nadia, having gathered that the nub of the play was based on some misunderstanding, and asked her what this misunderstanding was. This led to a further misunderstanding in that Nadia mistranslated 'sparrows' as 'screws' so I sat through the first half of the play in a Beckett-like state, thinking the telegram read 'two hundred barrels of salted screws', which made me think that Russian humour was just a little bit stranger than I had ever imagined. I felt something wasn't quite right. In the interval, I asked Nadia the significance of these screws.

'Well,' she said, 'they don't fly in that region.'

By this time I thought I had gone completely mad.

'Screws?' I enquired.

'Yes,' she said, 'screws.'

'Scrooooows?' I reiterated.

'Yes scrooooooows . . .' she said somewhat exasperatedly, flapping her arms up and down. 'Screws, screws,' she repeated. Then it hit her. 'Oh no, I mean sparrows.'

This was just another layer of the warm blanket of incomprehension that surrounded me on these visits.

Sunday, my last day, was 1 May. I had to wait in my hotel because of the parade, which finished at the doors of the Rossiya. On such holidays in Moscow it is impossible to move without a special pass. Of course, everybody had forgotten about the May Day Parade – and that the *angliiski actyor* was staying at the Rossiya – which was at the end of Red Square – where the May Day Parade would finish – and that he had a run-through of *The Crucible* at Tabakov's Studio – which was right on the other side of town – and that he had to catch a plane at six o'clock that afternoon. So what else was new?

From the buffet on the eighth floor of the Rossiya, I had the rare view of the exit point of the paraders, the spot where all the performers converged and mingled, having completed their various turns. I tried to open the window of the buffet to get a better angle for my camera. It was firmly shut in my face by a rather faceless gentleman.

'*Nyet, nyet,*' he said in his most emphatic Russian. Obviously a member of the KGB. At twelve-thirty Masha finally arrived, having made an endless detour to reach the hotel, and escorted me through more endless cordons along the parade route to the Tabakov Studio. As we walked through the streets in the aftermath of the parade, the marchers were beginning to disperse and to go home. Some of them were quite drunk, the younger of them singing current Soviet pop songs. At first it seemed so incongruous after the pomp of the parade, but then on reflection I thought, why not, they're happy? It was a bit like Whitehall after the Trooping of the Colour. Again, it occurred to me that this was just another example of similarities between peoples, as opposed to their differences.

At one o'clock we arrived at the Studio to be greeted by Tabakov. He had arranged for the rehearsal to be videoed. As at the Actors' Club on Gorki Street on my previous visit, there was an invited audience, much smaller than before, of about twenty people, this time mostly fellow students and friends. I hoped this would not put an unnecessary pressure on the cast and that they would not be strained to perform. 'Hell,' I thought to myself, 'I have only had twelve days to prepare and they're nowhere near performance pitch yet.'

In the anteroom at the side of the main rehearsal room where the run-through was to be held, I told the cast not to be concerned with trying to attempt a performance. This was still work in progress and today was merely a further stage in that process.

At one-thirty the run-through began. As was to be expected, the kids were nervous. But they had a lot of the play under their belt already and, after an uneasy start, settled in to some extremely concentrated playing. As the first act progressed, it seemed more than ever nonsensical to exclude Tituba from the act. But how could I have Tituba in the production as there were no black people in Moscow? It would be ridiculous, I still thought, and insulting to have one of the Russian students black up. In the interval, Tabakov offered a solution.

'Brian, this is no problem,' he said. 'We can get an African student from the Patrice Lumumba University in Moscow to play the part.'

Of course, why hadn't I thought of that? Silly old me. The Patrice Lumumba University. Of course!! Only I had never heard of, nor had anybody ever mentioned to me, the Patrice Lumumba University. Suddenly there was the possibility of having a Russian-speaking black in the production. I considered that for a moment. I turned to Tabakov and asked, 'Do you think you could possibly get me a Russian-speaking West Indian?'

Tabakov gave me a very old-fashioned look.

At three-thirty, the run finished. The kids were very depressed. None of them thought it had gone well. I told them not to be despondent.

Tabakov said he was very pleased about the level they had reached, and in such a short period of time and, of course, that he was aware that there was much more work to be done. He said that he wanted the work to continue and to be presented as a diploma performance in October when I would return to finish the production. There was a murmur of excitement among the kids. Then, with a great actor's flair for a theatrical coup, he told them about the trip to London in September. I shall never forget the faces of the kids at that moment. Despondency evaporated. Suddenly it was Christmas. The excited murmurings increased.

'We can work on,' said one.

'Three weeks in London,' said another.

'Two more in Moscow,' said the third.

After a session of notes, we retired to the Studio office where I was treated to my second farewell-to-Moscow party within six weeks. Russian champagne and delicious dried herring from Sakhalin Island courtesy of Igor Kozlov who played Hawthorne. His family were fisherfolk in that area, so from time to time they would send him a parcel of local delicacies. Apart from the students all the dramatis personae involved over the last twelve days were present – Nadia and her daughter and husband, Alice and Valery (Valery was a composer who in time would compose the score for *The Crucible*); Gerasimov, the Dean of the acting school, and the melancholic Masha; Sasha and red-headed Serge, who had attended a lot of rehearsals as observers and who very much represented the two ends of the scale in the theatre business anywhere. Both graduates of the school, Sasha was working in Tabakov's company as actor and director and Serge had been unable to gain employment since he had left the school over a year and a half previously. Mine host himself, Tabakov, was presiding and smiling as genially as ever.

Then at the last moment, just as my taxi had been ordered, Kutzevalov the designer arrived with the set designs for the production. Tabakov reiterated that they would have to be at the MXAT scenic workshops at the latest by the end of July. I had twenty minutes to consider them. I protested that it was impossible to make such a decision in so short a time. I rejected the design for Act II but thought that the designs for Acts I and III were excellent. Act IV naturally had yet to be completed. Kutzevalov had done these designs in twenty-four hours. Suddenly, I felt a resurgence of excitement in the production. I too had been despondent about the afternoon's run, feeling that there was a severe lack of visual detail. The designer and I talked frantically. Yes, he would do this. Yes, he would consider a solution to that. Throughout the rehearsal time it had been impossible to get access to material about the historical period of *The Crucible*. Only in the latter days had we managed to gain access to the library at the American Embassy. I urged Kutzevalov and Masha to follow up the contact we had made and get as much material as they could. In the meantime I would send material by diplomatic bag from London, working through the British Embassy. There was a quarter of an hour to go. The taxi meter was ticking away. As the party proceeded, the customary toasts were again exchanged, but this time there would be no sadness at parting. We would meet again in London in September.

Outside in the courtyard of the Studio photographs were taken. Tabakov and the students, myself and the students, Tabakov and myself. Again, as before, presents were exchanged. The generosity was overwhelming. Suddenly, Nadia was at my elbow.

'Brian, you must go, now. You will miss your plane. Masha will go to the airport with you. I must write letters about our trip. Here is my phone number. Ring me Tuesday, no, no, Wednesday. Masha hurry up. You must go.'

She bustled me into the taxi. I waved farewell and within seconds all had receded into the Moscow side streets. In the taxi, Masha and I gathered the loose ends of the day's rehearsal. I furiously began to give her a list of tasks that would have to be completed before we next met. The translation would have to be looked into, particularly Proctor's speech at the end of Act II. I wanted the designer to see a run-through, which would have to be organised. Final notes for the actors: that I wanted Apeksimova to be more poised; Ekimov as Parris should not dissipate his energy in the first act. Thinking back to my feeling about the lack of visual detail, it suddenly struck me that as the play was so unknown in Russia, an image or a sound or both should be used for the opening of the play. Suddenly there was a flood of ideas. A sound of young girls giggling, the image of shadows in the twilight, perhaps figures dancing by candlelight, a girl's naked back, the face of Tituba staring into the night. With this montage in mind, I asked Masha to encourage Valery, the composer, to explore a wide variety of scoring ideas . . .

When we reached Sheremetyevo Airport, a sudden awkward silence descended. The terminal was deserted. Masha and I walked towards the customs desk. I had suddenly run out of things to say. My impending departure had induced in me a kind of clumsy shyness.

'Brian, I have to say goodbye here. It is not permitted for me to come any further,' said Masha.

'Oh yes, I'm sorry, I forgot.'

I kissed her on the cheek.

'Goodbye, Masha.'

And she was gone.

*

On the plane was a group of young American teenagers who were complaining about the lack of decent food during their school trip to Moscow. When the British Airways dinner arrived, a few of them exclaimed, 'Gee, at last something decent to eat.' I thought to myself, 'Well kids, I don't know about you, but I've had a feast.'

Fourteen

I was met at Heathrow by Carolyn Sands. Our conversation as we drove into London mirrored the frenetic one I had had three hours earlier with Masha in the taxi to Sheremetyevo Airport. I had just completed my fourth trip through the Iron Curtain. That first journey I had relished as a pioneer travelling into unknown terrain. I now felt like a daily commuter on the 125 between London and Manchester.

Carolyn's enthusiasm for the student exchange was instant. The possibility of such an exchange had been discussed when the idea of my going to Moscow was first proposed. But it had seemed remote and ambitious and was not to be pursued until some time in the future. But the spectre of the idea which had loomed before me in Moscow now felt tangible. I believed that students of whatever nation would learn much more about art and culture from a first-hand communal experience of whatever reciprocal society was prepared to welcome them. Of course exchanges had taken place before, but the philosophical element of these exchanges had not been emphasised as rigorously as they might have been.

The problem, particularly in Great Britain, is the lack of vision in the policy of educating our young people by succeeding governments, of whatever political persuasion. Education in our environment is an embarrassment and has been so since time immemorial. The very notion of student exchange programmes is small beer in the priorities of education administration. It is left to a few individuals to forge ahead. Unfortunately, most of these individuals are chasing after the same small thimbleful of money. One of the great lessons to be learnt from the Soviet Union, and learnt before the society is demolished, is the priority of education for their young. One can only hope that this aspect of Soviet life will not be swept away in the necessary changes that will inevitably come.

As we reached my flat Carolyn mentioned that Tony Branch, who had gone to the United States for a week, had given his whole-hearted support to the exchange. He thought it would be possible to bring the students to London under the auspices of BADA. I told her that I was uneasy about this idea since BADA, though a charity, still operated as an itinerant drama school for young fee-paying Americans. Though an international course had recently been included at the Oxford Summer School and Tony had been instrumental in bringing the Moscow Art teachers there to give masterclasses, the academy was dependent on the income from the fees paid by these young Americans. Also, the title, British American Drama Academy, implied that the link was British American, not Soviet, or for that matter, any other country that might become involved. I felt that a new independent organisation would have to come into being, which didn't necessarily depend on fees and would be wholly philanthropic. Of course, this would make life very difficult. Perhaps it was unrealistic on my part, but I knew we would have to find other means of financing this idea.

We had five months to prepare for the arrival of the Russian students. It was agreed that Carolyn would call Tony in the States as soon as possible. I bade her goodnight as she delivered me to my door and made my weary way up the five flights of stairs to my flat, completely exhausted. It was still Sunday. During the past eighteen hours I had seen the May Day Parade, nervously sat through a run-through of *The Crucible*, attended an emotional farewell party, flown to London and had set in motion plans for a whole new organisation. But before retiring to bed, there was one thing I had to do, which was ... to read Chekhov's *The Three Sisters*. I was due to start rehearsing it the next day in the part of Vershinin.

The Three Sisters was to be directed by John Barton, the *éminence grise* of the RSC. As a young don, he had directed a production of the play at Cambridge in which a young Ian McKellen appeared. The production met with some considerable success. A success, alas, not to be repeated in this upcoming revival. Barton had gathered a cast of the best of the young actors at the RSC. He had the luxury of a thirteen-week rehearsal period. His intention was to liberate the play from what he believed was its yoke of naturalism imposed by Stanislavski and his intention was to present it in the style of the Elizabethan open stage. His cry during rehearsal was that the play should be available to the audience. In his desire to liberate the play from one theatrical yoke, he merely shackled it with another.

It is true that when the play was first produced by the MXAT, Chekhov was opposed to Stanislavski's direction. In his letters, the dramatist fiercely criticises Stanislavski's tendency for overstatement, by his suggestion, for instance, that after Tusenbach's fateful duel with Solyony, his body should be tragically borne across the stage à la Hamlet. Chekhov insisted that *The Three Sisters* was a comedy. This was the note that Barton was determined to take to heart. The term 'comedy' is emotive and so much of its definition depends on the user. Chekhov, Stanislavski and John Barton perhaps do not share the same sense of humour.

In Chekhov's case, to understand his use of the word 'comedy', one must first come to terms with the man. Chekhov was a doctor first and foremost. He had a physician's diagnostic view of the human condition. Upon examination it could be bleak and humorous at the same time. He dissects human beings with scalpel-like precision. Biologically he understands the muddled complexity of physical day-to-day existence and, though he is acute and precise in his observation, he is never judgemental or prescriptive. His brilliance as a playwright is to allow his characters to speak for themselves, never condescending to or patronising them. For an actor, playing and living a part in a Chekhov play is a gift because his characters are so totally rounded and varied; as human beings they are completely incomplete.

Barton's trap was one of condescension, particularly in relation to the part of Natasha. Natasha is the girl from the wrong side of the tracks who becomes enamoured of, and finally marries, Andrei, the brother of the three sisters. She is described by Masha in one translation as 'a lower-middle-class vulgarian'. The three sisters' attitude to this girl can be seen from several different viewpoints. First of all, Natasha could be regarded simply as a vulgarian who has upset the lives of these three unhappy girls. Another view is that Natasha is a lower-middle-class girl who is patronised and ridiculed by three snobbishly pompous sisters who believe themselves to be the sole arbiters of good taste. So Natasha's progress through the play could be viewed as an act of revenge. Both views can hold and both views contribute to the nature of the play as a comedy. If Alan Ayckbourn was writing *The Three Sisters* he would perhaps set it on four different evenings representing four different viewpoints. In all of Chekhov's correspondence about *The Three Sisters* he expresses a dislike of unsupported generalisations about his work.

During my most recent visit to Moscow, one respite in my killing schedule was organised by Sergei Ermish, administrator at the school. It was a trip to Chekhov's dacha in the country outside Moscow at a place called Melikhovo. This was the house where he lived between 1892 and 1897 and where he had written *The Seagull* and his novel, *The Black Monk*. Throughout the journey Ermish, a large jolly polar bear with tiny little pebble glasses and a handshake like a vice, spoke in non-stop Russian, completely ignoring the fact that I didn't understand a single word he said.

Melikhovo is a small farm of about five hundred and seventy acres, comprising the main house, a summer house, several outbuildings, and a large pond, built by Chekhov himself. In the main single-storey building Chekhov lived with his father and mother, sister and, from time to time, his youngest brother. The house appears very modest and the summer house, or *Feigel* house, is where he wrote and in times of the various cholera outbreaks, held his surgery.

Sitting in those RSC rehearsal rooms at Clapham the sheer smallness of the home kept flooding back to me, the tiny bedrooms, the small living-room, Chekhov's study, his father's bedroom with his violin and all the herbs that he used for his homoeopathic mixtures. The oddest thing about the house was its lack of kitchen. At one time it had a kitchen, but Chekhov could not bear the smell, so he had a new one built some twenty feet from the main building. In winter, with temperatures well below twenty degrees and as much as three feet of snow outside, getting hot food to the main house proved somewhat difficult. In a fit of temper, Chekhov would scatter the food on to the dining-room floor complaining that it was cold. The feeling of the house was domestic and homely. Our production gave anything but that feeling.

The read-through promised well. The cast had an empathetic understanding of their characters, even at this early stage. Nowhere was this more in evidence than in the refreshingly original reading of the role of Natasha by Pippa Guard. One of the many sadnesses of the rehearsal was to watch Barton subtly browbeat this excellent actress's interpretation into a condescending cipher and impose his own interpretation upon her.

I was very lucky to have been given some photographs of the first production at the MXAT in 1903. Also, of Danchenko's revival in 1941. These photographs were courtesy of the Moscow Art Theatre Museum, some of which had never been seen outside Russia. What is evident from these photos is the importance of the Prozorov family home and its changing face throughout the course of the action. As with any of the players, the personality of the house and its role in the play must be treated with the same deference and precision. I produced these photos at rehearsal in order to show the style of the period and the importance of the setting.

Barton misguidedly set the first act in the garden, completely disregarding one of the play's central motifs. In Chekhov's text the garden does not appear until the last act, suggesting that the three sisters have been dispossessed of their home, pushed out. Masha at one point says, 'I am not going in there. I don't go into that house now and I'm not going to.' The three sisters have been usurped in their home by Natasha. The first act is clearly set in the drawing-room. The sisters are in full possession of their home. Lunch is being prepared in celebration of Irina's Saint's Day. A party is in progress. Natasha enters at the very end of the act, disrupting the festivities. For Act II, the setting is the same, but this time Natasha has married Andrei, the sisters' brother, and is beginning to take over the home. There are children's toys lying about. The party spirit of the first act is temporarily revived only to be thwarted by Natasha. The third act is set in the bedroom of Olga and Irina at the top of the house. There is a fire raging outside. As the drawing-room was in the first and second acts, so now in the third, the bedroom has become the social centre. All the characters converge in this small room. The feeling is that the rest of the house is empty with Natasha well in control. At one point Natasha actually begs Olga to move back downstairs, which Olga ignores. In the last act we are in the garden. The pervading image is of the presence of Natasha driving the sisters and their tribe first from the drawing-room, then up to the small attic bedroom and finally out into the garden. When the play ends they don't know where to go next.

Throughout the thirteen weeks the sense of frustration grew more pronounced. Also the demands of the current repertoire at the RSC were beginning to be felt. Productions which had already played at Stratford were being revived throughout the rehearsal period. I myself was committed to travel to Tokyo at the end of May.

The project was set up by the RSC education department. The plushness of the Tokyo Regency Hyatt was quite a contrast to the formica finish of the Gostinitsa Rossiya. Four members of the RSC were to run a series of Shakespeare workshops with Japanese actors at the new Tokyo Globe Theatre. As it turned out, most of the actors we worked with were amateurs and Shakespeare as remote from their experience as Noh theatre is from ours. Nevertheless, they showed a touching care and commitment. The Tokyo experience was yet a further confirmation of the need for an international art exchange programme of the sort I had set my heart on founding.

During the second week of rehearsals for *The Three Sisters*, Tony Branch returned from America. He was unhappy about BADA not being involved in the exchange programme. With the backing of Carolyn Sands, I argued the need for a new organisation that would be non-affiliated and independent, working towards philanthropic ends. After further discussion, he conceded my point. Then the question of financing the new organisation arose. Fundraising was discussed, then discarded, as it would take longer than the deadline for the kids' arrival to raise the necessary funds through the channels of sponsorship.

'Why don't we do a gala?' said Tony. 'A special performance to raise funds?'

'Yes,' said Carolyn. 'Maybe the RSC would be willing to help.'

'Why don't you ask them if you could do a benefit performance of *The Three Sisters*?' continued Tony.

'That's an idea,' I said. 'I would like to involve the RSC in some way, certainly in the programme of teaching. I'm sure some of the directors who aren't involved in productions would be willing to take part.'

'On second thoughts,' said Tony, 'perhaps the Barbican is not the right venue. Maybe we need somewhere in the West End.'

'Well then it would be difficult to do an already existing piece of work, such as *The Three Sisters*.'

'Yes,' said Tony. 'We need to think of a theme.'

'What if,' I continued, 'what if we built the theme around the kids from the MXAT School? A sort of homage to *glasnost* and *perestroika*. Perhaps we can include some Shakespeare and Chekhov in the programme, representing the best of two cultures.'

By this time the idea was gathering momentum.

'What would be exciting,' I said, 'is if we had English actors doing Chekhov and Shakespeare, then the same scenes being performed by Russian actors. We could ask Efremov to release some of the Moscow Art Company for a few days so that we could present them in the programme.'

'Raising the curtain,' said Tony.

'What?' I asked.

'That's what we would be doing. Raising the curtain. A celebration of *glasnost*.'

'Brilliant,' I said.

'Perfect,' said Carolyn.

Tony went on, 'We should have some kind of compère for the show.'

'Who?' said Carolyn.

'Well,' I said, 'we would need someone well known, possibly with a reasonable knowledge of Russian and someone who is a confirmed internationalist, a sort of actor-diplomat.'

Then after a moment's thought we all said in unison, 'Peter Ustinov.'

Ustinov's past and continuing work with UNESCO was renowned. If we could get him to compère the gala it would be quite a coup and just the sort of profile we needed. I rang his agent, Steve Kennis at William Morris. Within twenty-four hours we had the reply that he was indeed interested and would be willing to meet us. A known tennis fanatic, Ustinov always contrives to be in London during Wimbledon. This year was no exception. We arranged to have tea with him one afternoon at the Berkeley Hotel.

We arrived just as the final set of the first day's play on the centre court was finishing. Ustinov cut an incongruous figure, dressed in a light-coloured suit, sitting in semi-darkness in front of the television set in his suite. A sumptuous tea was ordered during which his eye kept wandering towards a rather large piece of chocolate cake which obviously his strict diet did not permit. He was completely supportive of our ideas and said that he would help us in any way possible. But the date we had arranged for the gala would not be possible for him as he had to be in Leningrad attending a dedication to his mother. We quickly rearranged our diary and he agreed to act as host for the evening, with the understanding that if a lucrative job came up he would of course be released. In celebration, Carolyn coerced him to share the chocolate cake with her. He smiled in gratitude and together they demolished the mighty confection.

Things were beginning to move. The organisation now had a name, the International Foundation for Training in the Arts (IFTA). Tony had succeeded in getting a bank loan of £10,000 which the gala would refund. In essence BADA would sponsor IFTA. There were now two strands to the operation, the student visit and the gala. It was agreed that the gala would need a coordinator to organise the programme and the profile of the gala presentation, seeking advertising from various sponsors, etc. One name cropped up again and again, that of Anne-Marie Thompson. Her track record on such events was excellent. On the 23 June she joined our team.

In the meantime I had approached directors at the RSC to see if they would be involved in the teaching programme. I was able to put together the distinguished team of Bill Alexander, John Caird, Deborah Warner, Andrew Wade, the talented voice coach at the RSC, and the movement wizard, Ben Benison. Also, it was hoped to involve actors from the company in the classes. The directors would work with the students on a series of Shakespearian scenes. For the Shakespeare scenes the group would be split in two. For half of the day, the whole group would continue to work on *The Crucible* and the rest of the time they would be divided for their Shakespeare study.

The support from the RSC was wholehearted. The Old Vic had originally been at the top of our list as the venue for the gala but a clash of dates meant that it would be impossible. As a result of the RSC's involvement in the teaching programme, the Barbican Theatre now presented itself as the logical successor. A phonecall to the company's Administrative Director, Genista McIntosh, clinched the Barbican for the gala. We were now committed to Sunday 25 September, the last day of the students' course. The first priority would be to find a director for the evening. Again, the internationalist question was raised, which narrowed our choice. It was decided to seek the advice of the Director of the Edinburgh Festival, Frank Dunlop. Dunlop had a fairly comprehensive view of the international scene, his perspective would be invaluable. At our first meeting he offered to take on the job himself. I was a little surprised, knowing his commitments to the Festival. He said he didn't think this would cause any problem as the programme for the Festival would have already been arranged. So now we had a director.

The preparation for the students' visit forged ahead. As it was to be part of an exchange package, the funding for the venture was to be shared: airfares to England for the students would be paid by the Russian Union of Theatre Workers, IFTA would cover the other costs, giving them a *per diem* to meet their expenses. Their accommodation would be provided by host families. Because of the uniqueness of this experiment, the directors and teachers had agreed to work for a minimal fee. The group being split in two would necessitate the employment of a second interpreter. As the RSC had now moved their rehearsal rooms to Clapham, IFTA was very kindly lent the rehearsal facilities at the Barbican. (The irony of this was that the young Russians, who were used to the most primitive conditions, found the Barbican rehearsal rooms and facilities as oppressive as did the members of the RSC acting company). This was to be an enormous saving. A more than generous catering deal was worked out with Sally, the manager of the green-room canteen. Transport around London would be a problem.

The Friends of the RSC, who work so diligently on the company's behalf, came to the rescue. They made a considerable donation towards the cost of a minibus. London prices being what they are,

132

it proved cheaper to hire the minibus in Dorset courtesy of Carolyn Sands's local garage. The whole enterprise was run on the principle of 'I-know-somebody-who-knows-somebody-who-knows-somebody-who-wants-to-help.' The support was tremendous. Everyone we spoke to became smitten by the idea. Seeking accommodation, which we had anticipated to be the biggest headache, proved the least of our worries. Friends volunteered houses, flats, box rooms, garden sheds. The problem was to avoid having the students spread out all over the capital. Because of the flood of generosity we were able to concentrate them in one area, West London. The fondest memory for these young Russian people at the end of the day, was of those families who had so kindly taken them into their homes. I will always remember the tears at their departure.

The second part of this package would be the return, the following spring, of a group of British drama students from a variety of schools in the country. The criterion would be those schools that were accredited to the National Council for Drama Training. Funded on a reciprocal basis, the airfares to Moscow would be paid by IFTA in conjunction with the British schools, the costs of the teaching faculty, accommodation, *per diem*, and interpreters would be met by the Russian Union of Theatre Workers. It was my desire that, like the Russian students, the British kids would stay with families. But this was impossible, due to the lack of space in most average Russian homes. Though, when the British kids eventually did go to Moscow, they were met with equal familial hospitality.

So far so good. Incredibly, everything was falling into place. My main worry was that the uniqueness of the event would pass unnoticed. Tony Branch thought it was time that a PR company was involved. I was hesitant, but after persuasion it was clear that we would need a higher profile to capture the public imagination, plus it was vital for the life of future exchange programmes.

I pursued the idea of a documentary film of the kids. I tried the usual avenues, the *South Bank Show*, etc., but with no success. My commitments by this time were piling up. At the RSC rehearsals for *The Three Sisters* continued, *Titus* had opened to great critical acclaim and *Fashion* was enjoying a sold-out run in The Pit Theatre. My acting career was flourishing. The main driving force in my life, however, was to get the Russian kids to London. I had just about given up on the documentary when one night, after a performance of *Titus*, I was having dinner with my agent and a young independent film producer, Lavinia Warner. A proven innovator, Lavinia's work covered an extensive range of themes, from a drama about Japanese women in a prisoner-of-war camp, to a documentary of a lone woman's journey up the Amazon. I told her about the project. After I had finished, she said, 'Leave it with me.' Within four weeks, she had secured a deal with Channel 4 to produce a documentary about the visit of the MXAT students to London.

Fifteen

It was a year to the day since Efremov's visit to Oxford and I had enquired about the possibilities of travelling to Moscow. I was beginning to wonder what I had let myself in for. I was completely overtaken by events. Everything was moving at such a fast and furious pace. It was like someone with two tiny hovercraft engines attached to his shoes, permanently speeding at X knots per hour above the ground.

Anastasia Vertinskaya had returned to England to teach at Oxford, accompanied by Sasha Kalyagin. Efremov was absent due to his commitments in Moscow. I would spend my weekends at Oxford with Nastia and Kalyagin. Sasha was an ebullient, cherubic creature with a great sense of humour. His genius as an actor was dazzling. I had seen his performance in the Russian film of Chekhov's *Platonov*. He was a passionate and vociferous believer that actors should share their gifts with students. His position as the patron of the third-year group at the MXAT School was the cause of some envy among the teaching staff of the MXAT. Being a successful actor, his schedule was filled with performing in the theatre and acting in the cinema, but his great passion was for his students. He is an inspiration to all actors who wish to teach. During the summer our friendship grew.

My friendship with Anastasia was growing too. Personal relationships had been conspicuous by their absence for me over the past three years, and Anastasia was a constant reminder of a part of my life which was severely neglected. Our desire was strong, but in matters of the heart the cultural differences between us would, in time, assert themselves. For the moment, at least for that summer, we had an oasis of happiness.

Respite was all too brief. The demands of the RSC, the impending visit of the kids and the gala created a rising tide.

The first spanners were about to be thrown in the works. Peter Ustinov was offered a mini series which would preclude his appearance at the gala. He would have to pull out. The mini series, ironically enough, was Jules Verne's *Around the World in 80 Days*. Frank Dunlop's workload for the Edinburgh Festival had been greater than he anticipated. He would now have to forgo the directorship of the gala. A mild state of panic reigned. But, as always happens, out of bad will come good. The revered theatre director, Frank Hauser, stepped into the breach. An immense sigh of relief was breathed by all.

For four weeks Frank worked at a furious pace putting the programme together, ably assisted by the super-efficient Caroline Keely. Her clear-sightedness and precision meant that an enormous amount of time and energy would be saved in the coming weeks.

The Three Sisters opened to a poor press reception and I went straight into re-rehearsals for *The Taming of the Shrew*. After much phone-calling and telexing to Moscow, the formal invitation for the kids had finally been accepted. The whole group would come plus two design students, including Kutzevalov, the designer of *The Crucible*, Nadia as interpreter, Masha as costume designer and my assistant, and Gerasimov, who would be the 'father' to the group.

Matters were proceeding well with the organisation of the gala. Anne-Marie Thompson and her Stakhanovite workers had gathered together a formidable supporters' committee, chaired by Robert and Jane Rayne, great Russophiles and grassroot patrons of the arts. Dame Peggy Ashcroft, along with the Russian ambassador, Zamyatin, had agreed to be the presidents of the gala. At the age of eighty plus, Peggy is still one of the theatre's great pioneers. On the performance front we were still waiting for news of the Russian contribution. Invitations had been sent. By phone, everything had been agreed in principle, but without official confirmation we were in a state of limbo.

The bureaucracy of the Soviet system was driving poor Frank Hauser demented. It was difficult to conceive a programme until the players from Moscow had been finally confirmed. This hiccup aside, Frank was beginning to put together an exciting combination of excerpts from Bulgakov's *Molière* with members of the RSC, the star-studded current West End productions of Chekhov's *Uncle Vanya* and *The Sneeze* adapted by Michael Frayn from Chekhov's short stories, plus ballet excerpts from Tchaikovsky's *Romeo and Juliet*. Between them, Frank and Caroline even managed to find a balalaika orchestra.

With one week to go, I was convinced some disaster would engulf us all. I couldn't actually imagine the kids arriving in London. Throughout the last week the final preparations were settled. The timetable had been arranged for their classes, theatre trips had been organised, outings to Stratford and a visit to the American Museum in Bath for necessary background to *The Crucible*. Press, TV and radio interest was growing daily, letters were arriving from people wishing to contribute or just to observe the students at work. It was agreed that the last day of the students' course would be an open day for people to attend and witness the work in progress. Government interest was growing too. The group had been invited to a reception at the Foreign Office. I soon realised it would be difficult to steer the course of work because of these extra-curricular demands and it was important to avoid the kids being regarded as ethnological curiosities. The significance of the work had to be stressed at every opportunity. I would be torn by the need to achieve the highest profile possible and the priority of the students' studies. As D-Day approached my anxiety mounted, my nerve-ends were frayed like chewed string.

On the morning of 4 September I awoke from a restless sleep at about five o'clock. Throughout the night I had nightmares of plane crashes, students missing, revolution in Russia. As soon as the time was socially permissible I started telephoning, double-checking with all and sundry that the plane would be on time, that everything was in order. At times of stress one of my great security blankets is the telephone. My phonaholism during the Russian visit to London reached a zenith. My assistant, Virginia de Vaal, complained that having left me in the theatre after a day's classes with the students, she would arrive home to find my voice on her answering machine with some ridiculous query.

We were to travel to Heathrow in a convoy of cars led by Carolyn Sands. The students would then be chauffeured to a welcoming party awaiting them at Virginia de Vaal's flat in Maida Vale. That morning my son and daughter were with me. My daughter, Margaret, has a very clear measure of her father and had total grasp of my hysteria.

'Just calm down, Dad,' she said. 'They'll be there. Nothing will go wrong. Don't get hysterical.'

'I'm not hysterical,' I retorted.

'Yes you are,' she riposted.

I grunted.

There is nothing more galling than being disciplined by your children.

At twelve o'clock the convoy gathered at Heathrow. We had hoped to be able to use the minibus, but it was still travelling from Dorset. The tension mounted. It manifested itself in the series of body-hugging, self-deprecating, twitching hand gestures I suddenly found myself making. Try as I might, I could not break the habit throughout the whole day. Our eyes were glued to the arrival monitor at Terminal 2. Suddenly there it was. FLIGHT SU241 FROM MOSCOW LANDED. We crowded round the barrier at the arrival gate. I kept thinking, 'Until I see them in the flesh, I will not believe they're finally here.' The trail of passengers seemed endless and finally I saw a face I recognised. It was Kutzevalov, the designer, followed by Mashkov, 'Proctor', then another and another. Eventually all nineteen passed through the gate and onto British soil. Flowers were presented, hugs and tears and kisses and more hugs. The scruffily dressed, long-haired students I had met in Moscow had been transformed into young ambassadors dressed in their Sunday best.

The welcoming party awaited them in London's Little Venice. The sumptuous spread prepared by Virginia was eagerly devoured. Virginia de Vaal, a feisty American, was to be their 'in-house mother' during their time with us. Her no-nonsense warmth and tenacious tenderness was a source of challenging comfort to them all. When under pressure, she had a curiously comic mannerism of resting her glasses between her nose and her upper lip as if to say to any unwarranted predator, 'just back off!' At that party and their subsequent stay it was enchanting to witness the spell that the kids would cast over whoever came within their orbit. Their energy infected everyone who met them.

Soon it was time for them to meet the families they would be staying with. The minibus had arrived from Dorset in time for the party. Excitedly they bundled into it and were driven off to points west: Fulham, Hammersmith and Wandsworth. I had agreed to play my part as a host and have three of them stay at a small flat which I owned. My son would act as host to two others. We drove to a supermarket in the Fulham Road in order to get them some provisions. I left them there, gave them money and told them to get what they needed in the way of breakfast and an evening meal. One of the students was Valery Nikolaev, 'Danforth', who understood English quite well and would have no problem in purchasing the goods. I had gone to a garage to fill up with petrol. On my return I found them standing outside the supermarket with an empty shopping basket.

'What's the matter?' I asked.

'Well it's just,' said Nikolaev, 'it's just we don't know what to take.'

'Whatever you want,' I said.

'But how do we . . .' he hesitated, 'um, choose?'

'Just choose whatever you would like to eat,' I said.

'But *how*?'

'You just look at the shelves and pick whatever you want.'

'I don't think so,' said Nikolaev. 'Let's not bother.'

'Listen,' I said, 'go and get something.'

Sheepishly they turned away from me, walked to the other end of the store. After a few minutes they came back. In the basket they had beer and cigarettes. I sighed. Then I realised, of course, what a fool I was. They've never been into a supermarket. It's their first day in London and for the first time in their lives they have a choice and don't know how to make it.

'Well,' I said determinedly, 'unlike in Moscow, while you're here the one thing you've got to eat is fruit and vegetables.' And with that we raided the fruit department. Three weeks later, after they had gone back to Moscow I went into the flat and there was a bowl full of rotten fruit.

During the visit I became obsessed with their eating habits. If at lunchtime I saw one of them eat too many greasy chips and not enough veg I would pounce on them demanding that they eat more greens. I was determined that if they didn't go back to Moscow culturally wiser they would at least return healthier. After four days there were the first complaints of stomach ailments. Of course, I was poisoning them, this was probably the first time in their lives they had consistently eaten fresh vegetables every day and their digestive systems simply couldn't take it. I had turned into some sort of demented nanny. Persuaded to forgo the role of dietitian, I settled into the routine of the classes.

The first morning of the course I reiterated to the kids that they were young ambassadors of their country and that a lot of media attention would be upon them. It would necessitate on their part a need to discipline themselves to the work and the pressures of public focus. I realised I was demanding perhaps just too much. These young people were very vulnerable. All eyes were on them. They would be working in a goldfish bowl. In order that the work would not be disturbed I decided to include all distraction, be it the media or the documentary film that was to be produced, as part of the work process. There would be interviews, but these would be conducted in the lunch hour or when the students were available from rehearsal. I was determined that the work pattern would not be upset. It proved extremely difficult.

The day would begin with a round-up of the students by Joshua, our volunteer van driver. Doing the morning run from Wandsworth via Fulham and Hammersmith to the Barbican he would act as knocker-up for the kids. His day began at half-past six winding his way through the streets of London. Joshua was typical of the many volunteers whose generous contribution guaranteed the smooth passage of the timetable of the exchange. His close contact with the group and their tardiness would on occasion try his patience to the limits. Constantly on call, ferrying them from the Barbican to Clapham at lunch time, never once did he complain. His taciturn good humour carried the day.

On arrival at the Barbican, after the usually hurried breakfast, the students would start with a warm-up class, alternating daily with voice and movement. Then they would work together for the morning rehearsals of *The Crucible*. In the afternoon they would divide into groups and work on the Shakespeare scenes. The RSC also provided us with an extra rehearsal room in Clapham.

The work with the students was not the only priority in my life. I did have my commitments to the RSC and they were the ones that were paying my wages. *The Taming of the Shrew*, *Titus* and *The Three Sisters* were all about to open. There would be no let-up in this schedule until after the students' departure.

The visit was peppered with minor comic disasters. Tatiana Teslyar, diligently unpacking her luggage, discovered a set of false teeth, some heart pills and a few articles of an elderly gentleman's clothing. She had picked up the wrong suitcase at the airport. She was in distress. The case contained her entire wardrobe. Several telephone calls and journeys were made to Heathrow, to no avail. All traces of the missing luggage and the old gentleman, now minus one set of false teeth and heart medication, had completely vanished. To the rescue came Dame Peggy Ashcroft and Janie Rayne, who supplied Tatiana with both suitcase and a whole new wardrobe. The ironic end to this story is that on her return journey home, Tatiana again lost her suitcase and her new collection of clothes.

Since my leaving Moscow the previous spring, the kids had assidu-ously rehearsed the first three acts of *The Crucible*, unsupervised and in their spare time. Masha had been given the task of finding a Tituba. Prior to her departure to London, she had found two or three possibilities who were to be interviewed by Tabakov. Needless to say, because of his commitments he had not yet done so. So the Tituba situation would not be resolved until my return to Moscow. In spite of the July deadline for the sets, the designer had agreed with the scenic department in Moscow to submit the revised plans for Acts II and IV by 8 September which would allow four weeks for minor changes, the bulk of the sets having already been designed.

In the first days of rehearsal at the Barbican, Act IV was introduced into *The Crucible*. I began with a run-through of the work we had done in Moscow to which the act would be joined. The actors' performances had grown, with the exception of Ekimov who was playing Parris. The erratic nature of his playing was most evident in his anarchic approach to the first act. After the run-through I called him to task. He apologised and said that it had been impossible to work alone in Moscow without the help of a director. I too apologised, understanding his dilemma, but I added that I hoped there would now be a continuum of work until the opening in Moscow. He seemed reassured by this and, after two days of working on the fourth act, his performance appeared to be under control.

The work of Mashkov as Proctor and Shentalinski as Hale continued to deepen and develop. Mashkov's major problem was a vocal one. This weakness was shared by the rest of the group. The third act of *The Crucible* requires a great deal of vocal dexterity. I asked Andrew Wade, the RSC voice coach, to work with the young Russians on the text of *The Crucible*. Wade's ability to trigger the mechanism which would release the vocal tension of each actor and the young Russians' response to him in trust and relaxation was palpable proof of the validity of this exchange programme. I was able to witness first-hand what I had been preaching over the last eight months.

Later, in Deborah Warner's work with them on *The Tempest*, I saw further confirmation of my belief. She had created a magical atmosphere in the rehearsal room. Using instruments and their refined imaginative powers, the young Russians evoked a series of musical statements which could be held in reserve to counterpoint pieces of action throughout the play. Together with Deborah they created a multi-headed embryo which, with more time, would have grown into a dazzling production using a series of improvisations to explore the relationships within the play. In one example, Mashkov and Alyona, as Ariel and Prospero, improvised the creation of the storm. Alyona had insisted that she be allowed to play Prospero, breaking the sex barriers. Standing on a table she gathered her hair in bunches and gripped them with a hairpin beneath her nose, giving the impression of a handlebar moustache. She then proceeded to walk up and down, humming the march from Bizet's *Carmen*. Meanwhile, Mashkov had built a small model of a ship and positioned it at the front of the stage on a stool. His Ariel was rowdy and only communicated through whistles like Harpo Marx. As Prospero was marching up and down, in midstride he noticed a ship in the bay. He called for his trusty Ariel to invoke the heavens to storm. At that point Mashkov sailed across the stage on a portable wardrobe rail with wheels used for storing costumes. He had a bottle of wine in his hand. As he reached the stool, he spat the wine at the sailing ship, which seemed to have no effect. Then he pulled a box of matches from his pocket, struck the matches and threw them one at a time at the ship. Alyona continued to sing the Bizet march as fire and water rained down on the ship. The simplicity of this Marx Brothers routine brilliantly conjured up Shakespeare's *Tempest*. On other fronts everything was progressing equally well. The John Caird and Bill Alexander scene work was also flourishing. Bill's experiment of mixing actors from the RSC and the Soviet group had, after initial difficulty, found a common ground for the exchange of ideas in the reading of Shakespeare.

At the beginning of the second week a feeling of restlessness grew. At the official press conference organised to introduce them, the students expressed a worry that perhaps their workload was too heavy. The priority, for some of them, but not all, was the production of *The Crucible* and its success in deciding the fate of their future careers back in Moscow. It was indeed a diploma production and they would be judged on it by their masters at the school. I reassured them that *The Crucible* was my priority too. But the premise of the visit had been their exposure to other theatrical influences besides me. I emphasised how necessary it was for them to get an experience of work techniques which they might never have access to in the future; they might never come to England again, this could be a once-in-a-lifetime experience and they should maximise the opportunities presented to them in those few weeks. I shared their concern over the diploma, but the overall exposure to London and its people was something which no diploma would ever give them, an experience they would carry with them for the rest of their lives.

Work continued on the third act of *The Crucible*. Nikolaev was showing remarkable progress in the part of Danforth. It was important to maintain his confidence, to encourage the belief in himself as a figure of authority. The only thing that he lacked was Danforth's humour. It was the final door to be opened for him and it only budged after a great deal of trial and tribulation.

The choreography at the end of the act was beginning to take shape. As a group and individually, the prime intention of the girls was to win back the soul of Mary Warren, for without that soul the cabal could not function. Each had to sustain that intention through the antagonism of Mary Warren and Abigail Williams, and the accusations of John Proctor, in order to reach their eventual reconciliation. The manic state of their inner lives must be the source which disconcerts the court and, in turn, the audience. The act required an energy of playing which had to be frenetic yet controlled and defined. The concentration required would tax even the most experienced theatre ensemble.

With their new-found social life, burning the candle at both ends, the group was beginning to show signs of strain. Some were beginning to resent the interference of work with this new life. One morning, following a particularly disastrous movement class which half of them had not turned up for, I was forced to bollock them. When they complained once more that the workload was too great, I merely countered with my own workload.

By this time public awareness of the visit had taken hold. Press and radio interviews were being sought daily. The aim was to keep these to a minimum. The Russian service of the BBC had asked if it was possible to have two of the students on a programme that was broadcast nightly to the USSR. As it was outside rehearsal time we agreed. Shentalinski and Yulia Menshova (Rebecca Nurse) were chosen to take part. Months later, in Moscow, I visited Shentalinski's family. His father said, 'Brian, it was so strange. We had been told of the possibility of Seriozha being on the radio on this programme from the BBC. The BBC that had been regarded in the past as the chief agent of propaganda against the Soviet system. My wife and I sat down to listen. We heard our son speaking from a country three thousand miles away, a country which in my lifetime I never thought I would live to see. And this was my boy speaking on this programme. And for the first time, I had the feeling in my heart of freedom, that *perestroika* was possible, that *glasnost* was truly alive, that through our children travelling to the West, our worlds had come together.'

Sixteen

With five days to go till the gala night and the end of the course, Frank Hauser had reached an impasse with the gala. The preparation from the British point of view had gone remarkably smoothly and a formidable group of performers had been enlisted to appear, but there was still no news from the Russian front. Confirmation had not yet been received of the five Soviet actors who were to take part. This was causing considerable concern. Until we knew exactly who was coming and what was being performed it was impossible to complete the programme. The usual bureaucratic chaos was apparently in full flow in Moscow. The problem was between the Union of Theatre Workers and the Ministry of Culture, each vying for the kudos of submitting actors for this unique event. The only party benefiting from this stalemate was British Telecom, with the amount of urgent calls to and from Moscow. A compromise was finally agreed between the Ministry of Culture and the Union of Theatre Workers and a telex was received to say that the formal invitation to the actors had been accepted. They were to arrive two days before the gala and would include Tabakov (naturally), Natalia Gundareva, a leading actress from the Mayakovski company, Oleg Yankovski, the Russian film star, and Borisov and Vertinskaya, who would perform a scene from *Uncle Vanya*.

On the night of their arrival, I was to meet them at a restaurant. I arrived there to find Frank Hauser in a state of mild consternation – there appeared to have been an international incident. Gundareva had prepared a long monologue from an obscure – by our standards – Russian play, which Frank suggested as tactfully as he could was totally unacceptable for the gala. Gundareva was sulking. Yankovski, who had gone off into the night, wished to show an excerpt from Tarkovski's film *Nostalgia*, in which he played the central role. The cost of sound projector and screen hire naturally prevented its inclusion in the evening. Vertinskaya, exercising all her charms, persuaded him to perform the excerpt on stage; he reluctantly agreed.

Meanwhile Tabakov, pouring oil on troubled waters, convinced Gundareva that it would be wonderful for the London audiences to see a snatch of her triumph in Ostrovsky and that a perfect partner for her in the scene would be young Mashkov (John Proctor). She was seduced. God was in his heaven again.

Diplomatic relations were resumed.

In the final run-up to the gala the obstacles seemed to be coming thick and fast. Anne-Marie Thompson reported a distinct lack of movement at the box office. We were at that time in the middle of a postal strike and any requests or cheques for tickets could neither be received nor sent. It would mean a last-minute campaign to alert the public via newspapers, radio and TV.

The course was coming to its conclusion. Open days had been arranged as a finale. The attendance was quite phenomenal. Russophiles and theatre buffs came from as far afield as Cornwall in the west and Sheffield in the north. What we had achieved in three weeks with the people who had been in such close contact with these young people was a heightened awareness of the changing spirit in the USSR which heralded events that were to happen within the next year. For many the work at the Barbican was the beginning of the thaw of the long Russian winter.

On the eve of the penultimate open day, Virginia de Vaal collared me as I rushed via my dressing-room to the stage, still getting into costume for whatever performance it was that particular evening. This was a regular nightly occurrence – not having met me during the day she would buttonhole me to make decisions on outstanding business. That evening, in her feisty manner, she sprang this announcement:

'Kenneth Baker's coming to the open day.'

'What!' I said.

'The Minister of Education, Kenneth Baker, is coming to the open day tomorrow.'

'What for?'

'You invited him.'

'Did I?'

'Yes.'

'What should I do with him?'

'Nothing,' she said. 'Just let him sit and watch. He probably wants to pick up a few tips for his forthcoming visit to Russia.'

Of course it would be quite a coup to have the Minister of Education giving sanction to the exchange programme. At that stage in the proceedings the level of my tiredness was such that I didn't immediately recognise the significance of such a visit. With security in tow he duly arrived. Baker showed great interest in the students' work. The following week there was a photograph in the *Morning Star*, the communist newspaper, of Mr Baker holding a script of *The Crucible* and myself, mouth open, finger upraised, with the caption underneath 'The Lesson'.

The London rehearsals for *The Crucible* finished with a flourish of parties. The kids were now on a permanent high. For the next forty-eight hours the gala would take priority. Three of the boys under the tutelage of the prolific Mashkov had prepared a musical Brecht piece to be performed in the gala, entitled *The Poker Players*. The whole group would then sing a Russian folk song led by Ravyl and Menshova. Frank Hauser had been completely reassured of the Russian contribution to the evening. Egos had been stroked and put gently back in place. When asked the reason for his assurance he said, 'Well I have to confess when I challenged them about the length and suitability of their pieces I immediately feared they would turn tail and take the first flight back to Moscow; but then I thought, 'Wait a bit, they won't do that, after all, they've come here to shop.' He comforted himself with the idea that Oxford Street would win the day for him.

On the day of the gala, the behaviour of all, Russians and Brits, was exemplary. The British contribution was formidable, with such luminaries as McKellen, Bates, Tutin, Scales, West, Atkinson, Aitken, etc., and Jonathan Pryce and Imelda Staunton mirroring the Russian *Uncle Vanya* with their English version. Frank handled the technical rehearsal with the wit and the cool-headed dexterity of the seasoned professional. The atmosphere backstage and throughout the theatre was exuberant and responsible. No tantrums, everyone standing by and ready to perform on time. Front of house, Anne-Marie had marshalled the troops; postal strike notwithstanding, with the media's aid there were queues at the box office, the house would be full, with Lords Whitelaw, Gowrie and Lever in attendance and of course Dame Peggy and His Excellency, the Russian Ambassador, L. M. Zamyatin.

The RSC came up trumps with backstage staff and friends. Throughout the day the Friends of the RSC supervised a running buffet. Of course the seeming order was threaded with panic. The technical rehearsal finished an hour before the gala started, so there wasn't time for a dress. The actor Tony Britton's father had died, meaning that he would be unable to fulfil his role as dual compère with Tabakov. At the eleventh hour yours truly was ordered to fill the breach. The evening began with a 'hands-across-the-sea' greeting between Tabakov and myself, followed by the improbable balalaika trio. As item succeeded item, the sense of historic occasion was reinforced, the contrast of the Chekhov scenes in both languages, Shakespeare performed in Russian, and the music of Tchaikovsky's *Romeo and Juliet*. The form of the evening had perfect symmetry, despite the hiccups. In the excerpt from Tarkovski's *Nostalgia*, the character played by Yankovski has been asked by his dead friend to carry a lighted candle across the Roman baths at Bagno Vignoni. Yankovski was unable to get the candle to light; he succeeded on the third attempt only to have it blown out before he reached his destination. When this happened all of a sudden he went back to the beginning and started all over again. Meanwhile, offstage, I was narrating, trying to synchronise my text to his movements. When he finally arrived, he had to place the candle in front of him and say his only line. As he did so the candle again blew out and he said his line in darkness. Of course the audience was unaware that anything had gone wrong. They were totally mesmerised by the power of Yankovski's desperate concentration.

Then came the turn of Tabakov. He elected to perform the letter scene from *Twelfth Night*, playing the part of Malvolio. His performance had caused a minor sensation when it was first performed at the Sovremennik theatre some fifteen years earlier. Tabakov appeared wearing the most outrageous costume. The great champion of Stanislavski wore a wig that would not have even graced an amateur production of *Richard III*, tights that had toured one too many one-night stands in Outer Mongolia, the total look was that of Max Wall at his sartorial worst. As to the text, well ... only the Russian speakers in the audience would realise that it bore not even the slightest resemblance to the words of William Shakespeare.

But the stars of the evening were undoubtedly the students. Mashkov triumphed with Gundareva in the Ostrovsky scene, to be followed by his outing with Shentalinski, Ekimov and Nikolaev performing the Brecht with a dazzling range of their abilities, dancing, singing and acting in harmony, reminiscent of the combined talents of Kelly and Astaire in those early MGM musicals. The best advertisement for the evening an audience could have. In the finale the whole group sang with a rawness that touched the heart of every member of that audience. Peggy Ashcroft when she arrived on stage to give the farewell was still overcome by their song. The final moment of the evening was a moment of reconciliation. The great Russian director, Yuri Lyubimov, who had defected to the West during the waning Brezhnev years, had been invited by us to meet his estranged colleagues once again in public. The idea was a good one and milked for all it was worth by the Russians, but the following day on his way to the airport Tabakov was heard to remark, 'Why was *he* invited?'

At the end of the performance I was grabbed by the students and tossed by them into the air, each toss hurling me higher and higher. On the fourth I thought I would never see the ground again. Afterwards celebrations went on until the wee hours of the morning. I abandoned ship early and made straight for my bed. I knew that the morning would bring tearful farewells between the kids and the families that had so warmly taken them into their homes. For me, who had witnessed so many farewells and reunions with them, this was one I could afford to miss, for in a week's time we would see each other again, ready to complete the last lap of *The Crucible* and the final act of the Salem to Moscow journey.

Seventeen

My return to Moscow had been heralded by an invitation from the Union of Theatre Workers to my colleagues who had been involved in the students' programme – Bill Alexander, John Caird and the voice teacher Andrew Wade – to attend the first night of *The Crucible* in Moscow. The arrangements had been made prior to my departure.

Queues of families travelling on to Calcutta and Karachi, burdened with their in-flight cache of electrical goods, microwaves, CDs, cassette recorders, etc. crushed round the Aeroflot check-in desk at Terminal 2 Heathrow. The smell in the tourist class of Flight SU242 to Moscow had the pungency of the market of Old Delhi with its blend of sandalwood and garam masala. In the departure lounge I had made the acquaintance of one A. Craig Copetas.

Craig was Moscow correspondent for *Regardez* magazine in Washington on attachment to *Ogonyok*, the political journal of *Pravda*. This was his second tour of duty. A mixture of the genuine innocent optimism of a seventeen-year-old college freshman and the dyed-in-the-wool cynicism of the hard-bitten news-hound, his sanguine flair for resolving a story, however improbable, would come to my rescue in the final hours of this visit. We found seats together towards the rear of the plane. Due to the hair-raising condition of our aircraft, we fantasised about the role of the crew, imagining there to be two crews, one responsible for in-flight service, the other for the overall ambience of Aeroflot insecurity, seconded by the 'Department of Flight Paranoia' – the Khrushchev twins, strapped to each wing-tip with torches in hand, shining a path through the clouded night sky; Ivan the sound-man, playing ancient recordings of the creaking battleship *Potemkin* through the aircraft tannoy system; the giant Andropov, lying full-length along the top of the plane, whose enveloping arms, on cue from the pilot, would shake us in confirmation of turbulence; the monstrous Igor, sitting below us in the fuselage, repeatedly kicking the wheels of the plane into position for landing.

On arrival I was met by Anastasia Vertinskaya and driven to the Hotel Ukraine. As we were driving I noticed that there were no windscreen wipers on the car. When I asked her why this was, she replied, 'Windscreen wipers are a very precious commodity in Moscow – too precious to leave on the windows. In the past a great hobby for the Muscovites was to remove the wipers from the cars of their fellow citizens – the custom now is to use windscreen wipers only on very special occasions, the best example being when it rains.'

With that explanation, we drove on. I was back in Russia.

The Hotel Ukraine was the last of the so-called 'wedding-cake' buildings to be built after Stalin's death. Now on my fourth hotel, I had reached the archetypal tourist dive with its some 620 rooms, a quarter of which were reputed to be KGB listening-posts. The KGB paranoia was something I had not experienced on my previous visits to Moscow. It had crossed my mind that perhaps Nadia, my interpreter, might be KGB. I quickly abandoned that idea for she was far too indolent. There had been a notion among some that one of the kids might be an agent but this was plain nonsense based on pure envy of the individual's position within the group. In the past, KGB-watching had become almost a tourist attraction – see the Kremlin, see Red Square, see Lenin's tomb and see who your KGB man (or woman) is. For the Muscovite, however, this fear is only too real; Anastasia Vertinskaya during our time together in Moscow would always be a little anxious about the curiosity of – whoever. A secret society breeds secrets. I have always found it impossible to keep secrets; in Russia I would never be able to play the game.

Among the kids the anticipation of my reappearance had dampened. There was much to do and the bonhomie which had been present in the past was muted. Perhaps we had grown too familiar with one another – my initial feeling at that first rehearsal was of unease but I quickly shrugged it off as a passing cloud over what would become a brighter build-up to the first performance of *The Crucible*.

151

Tituba was introduced, a girl of Cuban extraction. She had made one or two small films at her university and had shown considerable promise. Within an hour it was clear that the poor girl was not equipped to appear on a stage. She couldn't reach the level of emotion which Tituba required. With only ten days to go, recasting would be almost impossible so I was compelled to try and coax her into dramatic life, an uphill struggle. Leila, for that was Tituba's name, was one of a population boom that had been precipitated when Moscow had opened its arms to the Third World in the mid-sixties, a phenomenon that caused a great deal of sniggered hilarity among some of the male members of our group. When I probed further I unearthed a slender seam of Russian racism of which hitherto I had been unaware. The inference was slight but later I would expose a far wider fissure of intolerance.

The main priority was to admit Tituba into the production, which meant concentrating on Acts I and IV, putting Acts II and III on the back burner for the time being. Apart from the obvious problems of Act I, there seemed to be a general listlessness amongst the cast. Their energy, which had been so powerful back in England, had become unaccommodatingly dissipated. Petty bickering broke out about who should be doing what and when.

'You said that line standing over there.'

'No, I was standing over here.'

The listlessness gave way to unsettled nagging. Again I thought it would pass and that perhaps they were nervous about the approaching opening. Physically and mentally too I was feeling not quite up to par.

The technical schedule for our opening had been prepared. The production would open at the MXAT Studio which was situated above the MXAT Theatre. The sets would arrive and be assembled a full week before the opening, but the rehearsals in the theatre would continue unabated. Valery, the composer, came to play through the score for the play. The tradition in the Russian theatre, I was told in no uncertain terms, was to use music not as an accompaniment but rather as suggestively thematic. I felt that most British composers would argue the same case and that this was not something particularly endemic to the Soviets alone. Valery insisted that the score be used in such a manner. I had no objections – only to the overuse and overscoring of the music and stressed that the sounds it created should not in any way be concrete but in the main organic, whispering, sighing, giggling. Of course, we reached a compromise and during the technical rehearsal I would remove what I felt was simply superfluous.

In the rehearsals the atmosphere was becoming increasingly problematic. Quite suddenly it occurred to me what had gone wrong and what was going wrong: the kids were in effect suffering from withdrawal symptoms, withdrawal symptoms from the life in London; no longer were they in the privileged position of visiting ambassadors and celebrities. They were merely drama students resuming their struggle to become young actors and actresses. Quite simply it was a case of deferred culture shock. Anastasia did not think this was the problem. She felt it was something more profound, but her position, like mine, had given her certain advantages which cushioned the kind of deprivation the kids were suffering from, deprivation that was manifesting itself in confusion and resentment.

One evening at the end of a rehearsal of the fourth act, the boil that had been festering erupted. A third of the group suddenly decided that the act was unnecessary and that the performance should simply go ahead with three acts as it had done at the end of the May Day rehearsal. The rest were bewildered but a few felt equally passionately that the fourth act was important. I realised that I had a rebellion on my hands. I seized on what sapping energy I had left in order to focus the arguments.

'What do you mean, you don't want to do the fourth act?' I said.

Ekimov (Parris) had elected himself spokesman for the dissenters.

'It is melodramatic and unnecessary,' he said.

'What do you mean?'

'Everything is clear by the third act. Proctor has been made to confess in court his condemnation of the society and his denunciation of God – the play should end there. There is no need to go further.'

'There is every need to go further,' I insisted. 'The argument in the play has not been fully debated.'

'It is bad drama,' said Ekimov.

'No,' I continued, 'it is not enough for Proctor, simply because he is emotionally racked, to denounce himself and the faith of his

153

community. In the fourth act he is driven to understand his personal responsibility to that community and to the renunciation of that hollow faith to which he has given lipservice. The key line of the act and the play is when Danforth asks him to name names by revealing fellow unbelievers. Then he is cornered. He will even go as far as saying the words, but when it comes to signing his own name, he cannot, because all he has finally is his name.'

There was a silence. Nadia had of course been translating throughout. Ekimov looked at me and said quite calmly,

'So what? In Russia people sign their names away all the time. Why is it so important now?'

I was speechless. It was one o'clock in the morning. Exhaustion defeated me. In my tiredness I could no longer think. I dismissed the rehearsal.

Anastasia drove me to her apartment. She had prepared supper. As we were eating, she broke the silence:

'Why do you do this?'

'What?' I said.

'Why do you work with these students? You don't need to do this. You are a successful actor. You have a good career. Why do you wish to spend your time coming here trying to pursue something that is foolish? You must do what you can do, not what you can't. You talk about energy dissipating but you are dissipating it by trying to do too much. Why? There is no need.'

I lay awake the whole night disturbed by Anastasia's questions, trying to formulate an answer, but it was impossible. Why *did* I do it? It had something to do with faith, an act of faith, belief in the development of the human spirit, man's understanding of himself and his fellow travellers, the need to reaffirm the virtues of life, to rediscover eroded goodwill, to share with and learn from the mistakes of one another, to build roads towards the common good of all. Perhaps for those trying to live and operate within the laws of a repressed society these thoughts and aims might seem too impractical, idealised and non-specific, but for me it was like being in the dark and as your eyes adjusted you became aware of a faint glow of light – you crawled on your knees, looking for the source, but all you were aware of was the glow and the glow was leading you towards that source that creates the light.

Ekimov's argument required a much more tangible retort. I suppose Miller's preoccupation with Proctor's need to hold on to his name could be regarded by these young Soviet citizens as a moral luxury but it's a luxury that anybody should be able to afford. Could it be, though, that in a society which had lived a feudal existence for hundreds of years and where the bulk of that society had no cognisance of the moral implications of the valued possession of a name, a society which thrived on individual anonymity, could it be that when that society finally abolished serfdom, it could not cope with freedom and merely imposed one feudalism for another, a feudalism of the state, in order to perpetuate the bondage? Put another way, in Russia when the existing order had been demolished and sixty years of freedom followed, it led to confusion because for the individual it was easier to operate duplicitously against the governing order. Morality did not get a look-in: 'The government is bad and repressive. I have to live and exist despite the government. I pay lipservice but I can behave in a wholly mercenary and uncommitted manner, following a code of non-responsibility – they're not responsible to me, why should I be responsible to them or to my fellow man, who is as corrupt as I am?' So what are you left with? Answer: anarchy.

Eighteen

Tabakov returned to Moscow in time for the final run-through of *The Crucible*. By this time the dissenters had agreed to the necessity of the fourth act but only after much exhausting argument and debate. Their acquiescence was still only grudging.

We had successfully achieved an opening for the first act. The idea that had come to me at the end of those early rehearsals in late April was to create a prologue involving sound and images that would reinforce the play's structure. The prologue would show shadowy figures dancing by candlelight; the dance would be interrupted and the sound of the dancers screaming would rise, with the help of the composer, to a crescendo that would herald the Reverend Parris kneeling at the foot of his daughter Betty's bed. Of all the new work that had been introduced so far, this had been the most effective in capturing the kids' enthusiasm. As the final run-through drew near I feared the worst. The progress that we had made in London had virtually been eradicated: we simply weren't ready to open.

The run-through, with Tabakov and Gerasimov in attendance, confirmed my fears. The second and third acts remained at best only competent. Everything was in place but a spirit was lacking and the earlier passionate fire failed to ignite. Act I was a total mess. Leila as Tituba was plainly inadequate; the performance was so small as to be non-existent. Ekimov as Parris totally abandoned everything that he had achieved; his performance bore no resemblance to the one that together we had so painstakingly constructed over the last four months. He had reduced his character to a ranting villainous cipher. Vocally, the whole cast seemed extremely tired. The lacklustre playing of the last act was only relieved by the focused passionate simplicity of the playing of Mashkov's Proctor and Marina Kolesni-chenko's Elizabeth. Kolesnichenko, throughout the year, had proved the most stalwart of the group. She possessed an indomitable spiritual strength that would impress the most jaundiced cynic.

After the run-through Tabakov, Gerasimov and I retired to a small anteroom beside the theatre. Though Tabakov applauded aspects of the work, he was not impressed by the overall result and he was aware that the kids had clearly not recovered from the trip to London. I felt that the opening should be postponed if it was at all possible. Tabakov said that this was impossible because of the repertoire schedule of the MXAT Studio.

'They are tired, Brian,' he said. 'You are tired. But there is much to be done during the next four days – we will have to work together. I think it would be best if I work on the first act and you attend to the necessary technical rehearsals. Also, as to the girl Tituba, there is no time to change and perhaps it is not so important, but this boy – he will have to go. We will have to find someone else to play his role.'

'Which boy?' I interrupted.

'This boy who is playing the Danforth character.'

'Nikolaev?' I said.

'Yes.'

'But I think he's perfectly all right. I admit he still has a long way to go – one thing he needs to find is a greater sense of irony – but with time that will come.'

'No,' said Tabakov. 'He must be replaced.'

'But why?'

'In this country,' he continued, 'he is totally unacceptable as a figure of authority; he is far too young.'

'But he's a student, for Christ's sake!' I said, my anger rising. 'They all are and they're all far too young for the roles they're playing.'

'Even so,' he said. 'This is a diploma performance and it would be wrong for him to appear. It would not do him any good. It's OK, he will understand.'

The argument went on. I reminded him that he had seen Nikolaev in the run-through earlier in the year and had not expressed any concern. He was unmoved. I then went on to express my shock at the irrationality of Ekimov's performance and how it would be necessary to realign his work throughout the production. Tabakov conceded to my concern about Ekimov but said that he was a talented actor and that he could be brought to heel. We agreed a strategy for the next four days until the opening. The technical problems were indeed immense and would have to be dealt with. I would work in the theatre while Tabakov continued in the rehearsal room. The question of Nikolaev remained unresolved.

Kutzevalov had designed a set for maximum mobility. Basically it would comprise an open stage with a series of small sets for each of the four acts which would be assembled in the full view of the audience in the darkness of the scene changes. He had enlisted six young design students as stage crew to facilitate these changes. The production manager was Sasha Khachlov, a veteran technical teacher at the MXAT School. Andrei Borodkin was our lighting designer. Borodkin had designed a lighting plot which would concentrate on each of the small sets, creating a 'light curtain' effect to mask the scene changes. This would prove to be the most elaborate design that the MXAT School had ever produced.

By the first technical run-through the sets had not arrived. Khachlov informed me that they would be there that evening. With great economy Borodkin was forced to set his lights to the furniture. The actors arrived in their costumes for the first time. Masha's anachronistic designs plainly would not work. She had bitten on the imaginative bullet but what we hoped would release the play from the confines of period only resulted in a visual ragbag. Throughout the technical rehearsal I noticed a young man sitting in the stalls. After about two hours I asked Nadia who he was. She said that it was Nikolaev's possible replacement and I was to interview him. I told her to apologise to him and to explain that the pressures of the technical rehearsal would mean that I would not be able to do so. I smiled at the fact that he was indeed a young man and not the Methuselah that Tabakov had promised.

That evening half of the sets turned up, the other half were still unaccounted for. We had three days till the opening.

Sitting back in my hotel room, I decided to issue an ultimatum. I called Tabakov and told him it would be impossible to open on time, and that I needed to talk to him urgently about my future and whether I was to continue as director of *The Crucible*. Anastasia reinforced me in my confidence about Nikolaev's ability. A head-on collision could no longer be avoided. The following morning I arrived at the school early. Nadia was there. Her work during the last fortnight had been less than adequate. In all fairness, I think she was as exhausted as I was, but I emphasised that this morning I would need her to muster maximum concentration in her powers as an interpreter. It had been pointed out to me that until my arrival in Moscow Masha and Ravyl had never spoken English and had been pushed to do so because they were dissatisfied with Nadia's translations. Tabakov arrived and we immediately went into caucus about Nikolaev and my future. I explained to Tabakov, perhaps over-dramatically, that I had not come three thousand miles in order to commit spiritual murder, to destroy the confidence I had built up with a student over a period of six months and to sacrifice his self-esteem in order that the show must go on. My faith in Nikolaev was such that if the show went on without him, it would have to go on without me. Tabakov said that he felt I was being hasty and rash. By this time I was feeling quite passionate. I said to him that my priority was as a teacher not as a director and that the relationship with my students was crucial to the success of any work which we had achieved together. The effort involved had been a group effort, a group that had been gathered together by the MXAT. Each member of that group had surmounted the enormous difficulty of working with someone not of their language. It would be criminal at the final and most testing hurdle to jettison any member of that group. Tabakov reminded me of my loyalty to the others. I explained that being disloyal to one meant being disloyal to all. If one was sacrificed the experiment which we had embarked upon would fail. I would not budge on this point. He smiled sympathetically and agreed that the opening would have to be postponed. I must go on directing the production and the question of Nikolaev would be left open. For the time being he would remain. We agreed that the production would be postponed till the following month when it was due to return to the repertoire at the MXAT Studio. I checked my dates with the RSC and discovered by sheer luck I would be able to return to Moscow. In the meantime I'd continue to rehearse the technical side of the show while we had use of the theatre, then for the last few days I would rehearse the actors with Tabakov before going back to England.

Half-way through the morning's work, three familiar faces suddenly emerged from the gloom. It took me a full thirty seconds to realise who they were: it was John Caird, Bill Alexander and Andrew Wade who had been invited for the opening night. Oh dear, I thought. 'I'm sorry, chaps, we've had a few problems – the opening's been postponed.' They were remarkably unperturbed by the news. In the midst of the chaos of a technical rehearsal, Alexander and Caird, both seasoned directors, rubbed their hands in glee at my discomfort.

'Now you know what it's like,' said Alexander.

When I told them about the problem with the sets not arriving, Caird puckishly advised, 'Do it without sets.'

I could have killed him.

On the afternoon of what should have been the first night, the sets finally arrived. For three days our stage crew had been improvising with imaginary flats and bits of furniture. At long last we had the real thing, but our problems were not over yet. The intention was to include the scene changes as a development of the action of the play, and at the end of each scene a crescendo of sound would fracture and disperse the sets; the stage crew would come on, dressed in black, and change the scenery in full view of the audience. It was necessary for this to be achieved with the maximum of speed. Khachlov suddenly announced that it would be impossible to do the scene changes in time, that the sets as built were unmanageable; they would have to be reconstructed. As they existed, he argued, the scene changes would take at least sixteen minutes each. This was impossible, I said, they must take no more than two minutes. Kutzevalov the designer insisted that they could be done in time. The argument raged for over an hour. Periodically, I would say to Khachlov,

'Why don't we just try it?'

'Impossible,' he said. 'Impossible,' he repeated.

Kutzevalov by now was crying tears of fatigue – he had not slept in over three days. After an hour I pulled rank.

'Sasha,' I said, 'we will do the scene changes now.'

'Impossible,' he said. 'They will take at least sixteen min . . .'

'Now.'

Sulkily, he agreed. The standby was given. Music. Lights. Cue first scene change.

Music. Lights. Cue second change.

Standby. Music. Li . . . Cue third . . . and so on.

Afterwards I sat in amazement. Each scene change had taken no longer than a minute and a half. I summoned him to me.

'Sasha, you said the scene changes would take sixteen minutes or more. I asked for two minutes. You did them in half a minute less than I asked for. Now, I could understand you doing them in fifteen minutes, I could understand you doing them in fourteen minutes, or twelve, but in a minute and a half . . . What possible explanation can you have?'

He looked at me and said,

'It's simple. We did them quicker.'

Because of the postponed opening, I was able to share with my RSC friends one or two hours of sightseeing. In the Pushkin Museum I found the solution to our problem with the costume designs; on the walls of the Flemish and Dutch rooms were portraits of the exact contemporaries of the men and women of *The Crucible*. We dined at the Praga restaurant in the Arbat. The Praga was famous as the meeting place of Mao Tse-Tung and Stalin; they had dined in one of the large chambers and at the end of the meal dismissed their entourage, including their interpreters, and for two hours they remained in the room, each unable to speak the other's language. In my present trough, the irony was particularly poignant.

I rehearsed with Tabakov and the cast. I observed his technique which was literally to stop them on every line and demonstrate his reading of it to the students, telling them exactly what to think and how to do it. There was no question that his skill as a mimic was consummate; there was equally no question that the kids were wholly dependent on him for approval. I would chip in my fourpennyworth, trying to steer them away from a crudeness of playing. We rehearsed in Tabakov's office. The students would enter from the secretary's room. A farce would follow in which Tabakov gave a suggestion to a student, who would then go into the outer office where I would pick him or her off and change it. Occasionally my pals from the RSC would be sitting in the outer room observing these tactics with a look of total incomprehension on their faces.

As yet, we had not held a postmortem of the last few days. I was saving it till immediately before my return to England. I felt as if in a way I had become Tituba: a cultural outcast. Just as she had introduced the girls to a 'black magic' so I in my turn with my so-called 'methods', was perhaps regarded as a radical threat against the grain and philosophic principles of the MXAT School – but only perhaps . . .

Tituba, apart from Nikolaev, was still an outstanding difficulty. Doubt about Leila's availability for future performances and her awareness of her own inexperience meant that she was unable to continue in the part. She asked to be removed. Tabakov's suggestion was that one of the girls from his second-year Moldavian group should black up. This was totally unacceptable to me. On the penultimate evening before my departure, my American journalist friend Craig arrived at the theatre. I told him about the difficulties I'd been having. Eventually I got on to the subject of Tituba. He looked at me and shook his head slowly. He then looked at me again.

'I don't believe it. I don't believe it,' he said. 'I think I may have the answer to your difficulty.'

'Which one?' I said.

'Tituba. Now listen, you're not going to believe this, but the other night I was at a restaurant, one of these new cooperative joints, a Belgium-Soviet cooperative.'

'A Belgium-Soviet cooperative?' I repeated slowly. 'What on earth kind of food would that be?'

'That's not the point. That's not the point,' he said. 'The point is, at this Belgium-Soviet cooperative there is a floor show and at this floor show there is this chanteuse singing the songs of Cole Porter in English.'

'So . . .'

'Don't interrupt. There is this chanteuse singing the songs of Cole Porter in English, but do you know what?'

'What?' I said urgently. 'What?'

'She is black. This is Ella Fitzgerald singing the songs of Cole Porter.'

'Ella Fitz . . .'

'Not really, you jerk,' he said. 'But it's Tituba. Your Tituba.'

'Good God,' I said.

The following evening we made our way to the small Belgium-Soviet cooperative restaurant in the Arbat and there indeed was a small rotund black female singer, singing the songs of Cole Porter. After her set we sent her a message asking if she would join us for a cup of tea – it was an alcohol-free establishment. She arrived at the table. Her name was Nora. I couldn't believe my luck. Then suddenly I wondered if she could speak Russian. I spoke without letting her get a word in edgeways: 'My name is Brian Cox. I'm a British actor. I'm over here doing a production of *The Crucible* with students from the Moscow Art Theatre Company. I've been looking for someone to play the part of Tituba, who is a slave from Barbados . . . It's a very important role and as yet we haven't found anybody who would be able to . . .'

The woman stared at me uncomprehendingly. I started to repeat myself. She continued to stare.

Then Craig said, 'She doesn't understand you.'

'What!' I said fiercely.

'Brian,' he said, 'I don't think she speaks English.'

'But that's impossible. She must be able to . . .'

And suddenly the woman let fly in a burst of loquacious Russian. Craig looked at me as if to say, 'What do we do now?' Of course we had no interpreter. I didn't think we'd need one. I immediately rang Anastasia. Within ten minutes she had arrived. After a little conversation Anastasia explained to us that our chanteuse had been an actress who had worked in the Gypsy Theatre, a notorious travelling company based in Moscow; her name was Nora Ivanovna and she would indeed be delighted to appear in the production of *The Crucible*. It was settled that first thing in the morning she would meet Tabakov.

Only hours before my departure, Nora arrived at the school for her meeting with Tabakov. I left them together. It was now time for the long-awaited postmortem. I gathered the students around me. By now Nikolaev was aware of his position and also of my support for him to continue in the part of Danforth. First I asked Ekimov why he had changed his performance. He said he felt that he had not been playing the part correctly and had decided to try a new tack, which he admitted hadn't worked. He realised it had been a mistake and he would revert to his original reading. I then turned to the group and said, 'This has been a bad time for all of us. I think we were overtired and obviously the Fates decreed that *The Crucible* was not to open during this period. But I would only like to add this: it appears that we have lost trust. I think maybe this has been largely my fault due to the pressure of the last few weeks. I came here to teach, yet in order to teach there has to be a two-way process. It seemed to me that in this school you want to be bullied and browbeaten into work, you want to be told what to do at every minute, at every turn. You need to be spoonfed. This is the "system" by which you learn. That is not my way, not my system. I will not bully. I will not spoonfeed. I can only teach by offering you a series of choices. I can show you a variety of ways of realising your work, but I will not act for you. You act for yourselves. You are individuals, creative personalities. The contribution must come from you. There is no profit in my saying, "You will do it this way and only this way." The satisfaction for me is in watching you find your own way, your own individual paths towards creation. If you want to succeed as artists you have to take responsibility for your own destinies. You cannot expect others to carry the burden of that responsibility for you. If you do so, you will find yourselves trapped in a system which can only breed resentment, a resentment which can only dissipate your creative energy. If you wish to avoid such dissipation, just remember: you yourselves are the perpetrators of the system that created it.'

By the last day my British colleagues had returned to England. My relationship with Anastasia was drawing to a close. Conducting an affair over 3,000 miles would prove impossible and differences in outlook magnified. Whereas I regarded the artist's role as a respected one, a necessary contributor to the spiritual wellbeing of society, I could not agree with her strong belief that the artist should be venerated, accorded some position that transcended the common folk. In the cemetery at Novodevichy, for instance, a hidden élite of Moscow society comes clearly into view. The graveyard is ghettoised:

the modern part a privileged sanctuary for members of the Party élite; the older part a holy sepulchre for artists. The graves are elaborate. The simplest one in the artists' section is that of Anton Chekhov. I find any worship of dead artists instantly arouses the iconoclast in me. In Russia the struggle for existence is sharply focused: the need to create a cult of the actor or the writer comes from the lack of material wellbeing. Of course it would be easy from my position to perhaps sneer at the idolatry of the artist but if you live in a two-room flat with no proper bed, only a sofa-bed in order to give you maximum space, and decorate your small place with trimmings of grandeur in order to alleviate the gloom of your life, the fantasy of an elevated existence is a means of survival. But that fantasy can warp your perspective.

After all that had happened with *The Crucible*, it would have been understandable to have walked away, to have had no more to do with what was perhaps a hopeless quest. The one thing I feared most had happened: I had hit the seam of our cultural differences. I knew that I had to go on. The differences had been established, differences of conditions and environment, not merely through ideas but tangible facts discovered during close work. The last dregs of energy that I had left drove me on with the new-found knowledge of the barriers that existed; but they were just that – barriers. But walls could be breached. I resolved to continue. *The Crucible* would now open on 15 November as planned.

Nineteen

My arrival in London was followed by a flurry of activity even greater than before. The gala had established IFTA. The board of IFTA had sanctioned the second part of the exchange, involving the English drama students travelling to Moscow, but if it was to gain momentum, an administrator would be needed; Caroline Keely's work throughout the last few months made her the obvious choice. Caroline and I contacted the heads of the top drama schools in the country. They were delighted to be able to take part. We now had to plan a strategy for raising funds. IFTA required a seedbed of capital if it was to continue. At the moment there was none. Caroline was working on a part-time basis with a promise of deferred payment. The gala, which we had hoped would provide capital, merely broke even. Ill advice and the postal strike had not helped. The one thing we had achieved was a higher profile, but as to real money . . . it was time to rattle the begging bowl. In the weeks that followed, we wooed and brown-nosed our way through a range of possible channels, from banks to travel companies, any group that might have the slenderest connection with the arts, education or Russia. We made some progress but the struggle was not just uphill, it was perpendicular. Our successes were minimal, a Xerox machine donated by the Rank Organisation for the MXAT School. When I told Tabakov of this gift in Moscow, he paused, thought for a moment and said, 'An Apple-Macintosh computer would be good.' An annual scholarship awarded by the International Theatre Institute – these contributions were confidence-boosting but the overall effect of all the effort was demoralising. In the current political and financial climate we had no choice but to go on if only to find the one benefactor who believed in the principle of international exchanges. As yet we had not tried government agencies like the British Council, Arts Council, etc. They would be our next ports of call.

I was still working at the Barbican. *Titus* continued to grow and improve, *The Three Sisters* to regress. A possible European tour of *Titus* was mooted. The company were excited by the prospect of fresh air after the compression chamber of the Barbican.

Then came a call from Moscow: *The Crucible* would now open on 16 not 15 November. I was performing *The Three Sisters* on 16 November. This might prove interesting. Perhaps by then I would have mastered the art of self-division and be in two places at once. I could not believe this latest piece of news. I requested an interview with Terry Hands, then El Supremo of the RSC. I told him I realised my commitment was first and foremost to the Company but asked him if it was possible, due to the uniqueness of the occasion, for my understudy to play for me. I emphasised that in no other circumstances would I ask this favour. He was sympathetic and said he would have to consult the associate directors. I knew then that I would not be in Moscow on 16 November. In the meantime I waited in hope . . . and waited. I informed Tabakov of the likelihood of my not being able to attend the opening of *The Crucible*. There followed an historic exchange of memos between the Artistic Director of the RSC and the Principal of the Moscow Art Theatre School in which Tabakov did his best:

> It is impossible for me to overemphasise that Brian's production of *The Crucible* is essential for the life of the Moscow Art Theatre School. The energy and expertise that he has brought to the Soviet students who have worked alongside him in London and Moscow, as well as to the many actors and crew members whose lives he has touched, is beyond value. Brian's presence in our school has set a new precedent for what we will both be able to accomplish on our stages in the years to come; to lose him now would be a great tragedy for theatrical development and understanding in both our countries.

Terry's answer, explaining the British tradition of 'playing as advertised' and the use of understudies – for accident or illness only – continued:

167

Performing in England is rather like running the Marathon. It hurts like hell but you never quit because if you do it will hurt more next time and you'll quit sooner.

And ended:

Brian can be with you from 11 November without any problems – but on 16 and 17 November he has *The Three Sisters* – and Vershinin doesn't normally get to Moscow. I will examine the problem with my colleagues but you will forgive me if at the moment I cannot be too hopeful.

The angst of divided loyalties was further exacerbated. Deborah Warner had won the 1988 *Evening Standard* Drama Award as Best Director for the production of *Titus*. The *Standard* and the press office of the RSC were chasing me to do an excerpt for the televised award presentation. With the little time I had left before my return to Moscow, I was anxious to have some respite and in particular to see my daughter who had just recently started a new school and whom I had not seen since the summer. Ignoring the countless pleas on my answering machine, I made a hasty retreat to the haven of the country. Of course, on the way north, I was conscience-stricken and rearranged my cluttered diary.

After three days of walks and talks, I bade farewell to my daughter and returned to London and the unresolved question of Moscow. On my answering machine there was a message from Bill Alexander, producer of the Barbican season. The problem of Moscow had been placed firmly in his court. I arranged a meeting with him and withdrew my request to be released from the performances of *The Three Sisters*. I rang Tabakov and told him of the decision. He naturally understood. A new date for *The Crucible* was fixed – 15 January, 1989 – ten months after my first visit to Moscow.

My schedule for the five days in Moscow would include working with Nora Ivanovna on the part of Tituba and meeting with representatives of the British Council in order to pursue the return exchange visit. Tabakov had assured me that during my absence he would rehearse Nora into the production. To my surprise I found he had not done so. Only the consideration of Masha had kept Nora informed of her position. She had not acted for a number of years, having found work extremely difficult to come by. Since she had parted with the Gypsy Theatre, her only employment had been as a singer in various nightclubs. Her passion was jazz and her one great request was that I bring her the songbooks of the famous jazz composers of the thirties and forties. The mystery of Nora's origins remains – to this day. No one has ever explained her roots. At the first rehearsal she was extremely nervous, but I could quickly tell that she had a colossal interior strength. She gave Tituba an enormous dignity: here was a woman with a profound cultural background reduced to working as a slave for this inferior white preacher, a woman who could endow these young girls with mysteries of a hidden world, a world which would threaten the fabric of their lives. Suddenly a new perspective on the play was presented to me. I saw how an alien presence (Tituba) disturbs the set order, the theocratic order in the case of *The Crucible*, but also I was aware that the theocratic world is equally disturbing from the alien's viewpoint. This reinforced the fundamental impregnability of two cultures, mirroring for me, also an alien, the differences I was experiencing.

Nora's advent spurred me to a new enthusiasm for the brilliance of Miller's work. The resonances and parallels between what had happened over the last ten months and the material with which I was working was quite astonishing. The kids had been visibly shaken by the confrontations on my previous visit. And through the events of the last few weeks they were now aware of how the play mirrored the stuff and shape of their lives.

There was an air of euphoria about the fact that we had been given a second chance, and indeed it would have been impossible to contemplate trying to open in this period. It was a time to reforge links which had been broken, to renew our trust. Having re-established our mutual bond we could look forward to the opening in January. Tabakov had reconciled himself to Nikolaev playing the part of Danforth. I still detected a qualification on his part. From Nikolaev's point of view a rapprochement with Tabakov was vital to his continuing at school. My task was to bring this about. Tabakov would go on working with him after I left. I suggested he should bolster Nikolaev's sense of ironic humour. I knew that the road to finding their mutual confidence was to identify a joke which they could share together, something in which I couldn't help because the joke would have to be profoundly Russian.

At the British Embassy, I arranged a meeting with the Counsellor for Cultural Affairs. I told him all about the exchange programme. He had already heard about our work and showed great interest and enthusiasm. He asked me to prepare a paper which I should submit to the British Council in London as all financial matters regarding cultural exchange were dealt with by them. When I returned to London I submitted the said paper and, with Caroline Keely, set a meeting. The Council informed us that the matter of finance rested with the Embassy in Moscow, not in Britain. Again, they were sympathetic but said I should contact their man in Moscow. Apparently their man in Moscow wasn't the gentleman I had met, but another gentleman who controlled the purse strings: the Counsellor for Cultural Affairs was Foreign Office and the other gentleman was British Council and never the twain shall meet. Eventually, having spoken to a variety of ladies and gentlemen at the British Council and the Foreign Office in London, we got the money to finance the exchange through the Embassy in Moscow.

Twenty

When I had first arrived in Moscow ten months earlier, Mikhail Gorbachev's *perestroika* was in its infancy. By January 1989 it had grown into a precocious toddler, trying to find its feet, a toddler with no sense of danger, no awareness of hot or cold. Only by getting burnt could it establish the difference. The fingers of *perestroika* were now developing calluses. The January 1987 plenary meeting of the CPSU Central Committee had encouraged the redemocratisation of Soviet society at every level, to develop self-government and create greater initiative and genuine control from the workforce.

It was Year Two of a new history. The young men and women of the MXAT Theatre School were taking the policies of Gorbachev to heart. The very traditions of the Moscow theatre were being challenged. Efremov was finding it increasingly difficult to recruit new up-and-coming players for his theatre. No longer were the young interested in playing Nina and Konstantin in the fourteenth revival of *The Seagull*. They preferred new work in smaller intimate theatres or the cinema. Tabakov was sympathetic to Efremov's plight but also understood the new desires of the young people.

In the spirit of *glasnost*, Efremov had accepted the resignation of several senior members of his company – Sasha Kalygin, Oleg Borisov, and Anastasia Vertinskaya. They too, like the kids, wished to exercise a newfound independence. The average wage for a leading actor was then 450 roubles a month (roughly £400). They would supplement this income with forays into screen work. A great means of income for the star actor is to take part in what are known as 'concerts'. These concerts – really benefits in the nineteenth-century sense – would entail travelling to various parts of the Soviet states and appearing at a huge venue, sometimes a two to three thousand-seat auditorium, in a retrospective of his or her work; i.e., clips from various films interspersed with stage readings and a question-and-answer session for which the actor might be paid as much as 3,000 roubles. For someone like Tabakov these concerts were a great source of finance which subsidised the work of his studio.

The depletion of his élite core of players and the inability to inspire the young to join his company created a dilemma for Efremov. Obviously the MXAT would have to be restructured and align itself with the winds of change but in the meantime some kind of holding pattern was necessary to stimulate the interest of the audiences. Apart from MXAT, the studio was proving to be extremely successful, especially productions from the school. Tabakov came to Efremov's rescue. Quite simply, he arranged for the course of the drama school to be extended. Originally a four-year course, Tabakov created a fifth year which would play exclusively at the MXAT Studio. So whether they liked it or not, students would now be proxy members of the MXAT Theatre Company.

I was to visit Moscow one last time before *The Crucible* opened. But my memories come back to me for some reason as a fragmented montage: some work – but it was not always possible, with the uncertain availability of students; discussions of a film which would take place with the visiting English group; the introduction of others to Moscow, detachedly witnessing through their eyes all the traumas, bureaucratic nightmares, excitement, frustration that I had over the months experienced; the simple pleasure of travelling up the river by boat; walking in Gorki Park; Saturday afternoons with my American friend Craig Copetas; visiting the antique market at Ismylova Park, gathering a crowd in order to inflate the prices of some struggling artist's work. Queues and the forming of them are a great Soviet pastime: Ismylova Park is no exception. One Saturday our interest had been taken by some particularly garish paintings of cheeses. The *babushka* who was 'gardienne des fromages', explained she was selling these on behalf of her son who had reached a creative impasse and would no longer work but just hang about their small apartment in a state of blissful meditation. Unable to stand the situation any longer, she had seized his portfolio and come to the market place herself. In sympathy, parodying loud American tourists, we grabbed the paintings and began extolling their virtues: 'My Gaaad, look at this work . . . simply magnificent . . . galleries back home would pay a fortune for this stuff.'

Within seconds the crowd had gathered – we slipped away.

More fragments come back to me: the Pushkin Museum, to look again and again at the study of light in Monet paintings of Rouen Cathedral, Picasso's Pierrot; lunch at the Slavyanski Bazaar, haunt of Stanislavski and Nemirovich-Danchenko where their eighteen-hour conversation launched the Moscow Art Theatre in 1895, now under the guidance of the tiny dynamo Rosa Serota, great drama teacher of the Gorki Theatre in Leningrad and now the MXAT in Moscow; revisiting the Stanislavski Museum with the improbable designs for Gordon Craig's *Hamlet* on display. But the abiding memory is of the families I met: the Shentalinskis, Vitaly and Tanya, Sergei their son, Masha their daughter and tiny Arseny their grandchild; Vitaly, a writer whose burning passion has been the excavation of Russia's recent literary past, the recording and re-habilitation of those writers who had disappeared during the purges of Stalin. Sitting in the small apartment, he would read from T. S. Eliot and Masha and Tanya would sing pre-Christian folk songs of old Russia, while Arseny slumbered on his father's lap. These are the memories that sustained me and enabled me to leap the final hurdle of Salem to Moscow.

Twenty-one

The Minsk Hotel was to be my final home in Moscow. Built in the sixties, the Minsk was an eroded temple of G-Plan contemporary design. The windows in every room had an inch-wide gap between them and the brickwork – if that's not too ambitious a description – and the sill, providing air-conditioning from the sub-zero blasts of Gorki Street below. Occasionally, in some of the rooms, an attempt at draught-exclusion had been made, in the form of bandaging – no doubt from supplies of the Soviet Red Cross. Two days of living in a room with a chill factor of ten degrees below zero persuaded me to seek another. After much cajoling and wooing of the concierge, I managed to secure a suite on the leeward side of the hotel where the gaping windows were still the same, but the wind was blowing in the opposite direction.

This trip I had a new interpreter. Nadia had finally given up the ghost. She too had succumbed to the entrepreneurial spirit of *glasnost* and was now working as the would-be English/American tour manager of a Soviet pop group. She insisted on trying to foist tapes of this and various other groups on me to take back to the West. Each group was indistinguishable from the others, sounding like an amalgam of the Cassidy family and the Bay City Rollers. Out of anthropological curiosity, I attended a pop concert as a guest of Nadia. The memory is a blur.

My new interpreter was a rather nervous lady with a high-pitched voice, called Mila. Mila was the exact opposite of Nadia. As an interpreter she was excellent; as an organiser disastrous. She had no experience of the theatre and could only gaze in horrified wonder at the behaviour of the students. But her concern for my welfare was exemplary. Her mothering instincts meant that for the first time in a whole year there were supplies of tea and snacks.

The atmosphere for the final rehearsals was buoyant, though there was endless work left to do on the technical side. The sets, which supposedly should have been finished for the October opening, were still incomplete. Tabakov himself had paid for the building of these sets, no doubt from his 'concerts', at black-market prices, in order to facilitate their construction.

One morning Kolya, our soundman, summoned me to his sound studio at the school. On my last visit Valery the composer and I had debated the use of certain pieces of music. At the end of the play, after Proctor has gone to his death and Elizabeth observes him from the window of the cell, he had wanted to use a particular piece of music, a very early arrangement of 'Ave Maria'. I tried to point out to him how inappropriate 'Ave Maria' was to a group of early American Puritans. His argument was for the aesthetics rather than the accuracy of the moment and I could not get across the Catholic associations of the Virgin Mary which would be abhorrent to dyed-in-the-wool Proddies like the citizens of Salem, Massachusetts. Kolya had overheard this disagreement and through a misunderstanding obviously thought that I was displeased with the entire score of *The Crucible*. As we sat in his studio that morning it was soon apparent that he had completely rewritten the music. I sat stunned as he played piece after piece of what I can only describe as a cross between elevator muzak and the theme from *Indiana Jones and the Temple of Doom*. Finally we got to the disputed 'Ave Maria' piece for which Kolya had substituted a chant of what sounded like a Greek balladeer, much in the manner of Nana Mouskouri. After the music finished, I sat silently. Masha who was with me could not look me in the face. With her eyes to the ground, she asked Kolya who the performer of the last piece was. He said, 'It's a Greek balladeer called Nana Mouskouri.'

Supporting each other, in repressed laughter Masha and I staggered out of the studio. By this time in my adventure, I was beginning to see a few holes in the aesthetic fabric of Soviet culture.

The students were now united about the last act of the play. As is usual, the dissension over the fourth act had grown from the difficulty of the playing. The emotional demands for each actor were extreme. Proctor's awareness of his hypocrisy, Parris's terror of reprisals, Danforth's fear of losing control, Hale's loss of faith and Elizabeth's remorse for alienating her husband – for each actor, these were the final peaks to be scaled. Nikolaev, surprisingly, was enjoying a new confidence in his playing and also his relationship with Tabakov. Tabakov, too, took pride in his achievement.

After one particular run-through, he turned to me and said, 'This student is very good. Very good.'

'Yes,' I reminded him, 'he's the boy you wanted to get rid of three months ago.'

He smiled his puckish grin and shrugged. 'He has improved.'

During my absence Nora as Tituba, had still not been rehearsed. She was and remained very much the outsider. The resentment of her by Tabakov and the group was deep-seated. At one rehearsal, when she had arrived an hour and a half late, Tabakov turned to me and said, 'These people are very unreliable. The Gypsy Theatre is notorious for its disorganisation and internal squabbling. We must find someone else to learn the part. Who knows whether or not she will turn up for a performance?'

On arrival, Nora complained that she had been kept waiting and that the commissionaire on the door of the MXAT Theatre would not let her through without a proper pass. Some of the students had come through the door and claimed not to have noticed Nora's presence. Whether the story was true or not was hard to tell. Though Tabakov admired her performance as Tituba, obviously there was a racial divide that *The Crucible* could not bridge.

For the opening of *The Crucible*, the one person who deserved to be there was Carolyn Sands. Her support from the very beginning of the project had been unfailing. It was her just reward to see her efforts come to fruition. On the last day of rehearsals I worked for eighteen hours straight without even pausing for food. After running through the scene changes endlessly, timing the music and the lights, integrating them with the dramatic action, we finally achieved a synthesis in the production. Borodkin the lighting designer had done wonders with his limited resources. The young designers who constituted the stage crew performed the swift changes with breath-taking dexterity; the effect achieved of a shattering and reassembling world that created just the right degree of disorientation for the audience. The one remaining problem was this wretched piece of music to end the performance. I had wanted the sounds to increase and the sense of a bright red sunlight to burn through the slatted walls of the set, denoting the dawning of a new day. My composer still wanted to have bloody 'Ave Maria' as the final theme. I continued to resist. Finally Tabakov came forward with a compromise idea. He suggested the Adagio of the baroque composer Albinoni. I baulked at this suggestion; though beautiful, this piece of music for me is synonymous with an up-market TV commercial – a culture gap yawned. For Tabakov, the music remained the music; there were no associations with the hard- or soft-sell. Of course, the loss was mine. I could not get a Volvo ad out of my head. It depressed me to realise how desensitised I had become. The fault lay with my culture, a culture that had hijacked something exquisite in order to promote an automobile or a washing machine. A further compromise was reached. As long as I was in Moscow or if the production were ever to travel to the West, silence would prevail, but in my absence or on a tour of the Urals Albinoni reigned OK.

With diploma performances at the MXAT Theatre School, the final dress rehearsal before the opening is purely for the benefit of the teaching staff. It is the performance on which a student's entire efforts are judged. *The Crucible* was no exception. After the dress rehearsal a postmortem is held to which the director is invited to participate in the cross-examination. Again, *The Crucible* was no exception. As I sat on the stage of the MXAT Studio under the withering gaze of the school faculty, I felt as if I were seven years old again, about to attend my first confession, desperately trying to remember all the sins I had committed, hoping my penance would not be too harsh. First, the head of design thanked me, then cautioned Tabakov against such an ambitious project, reluctantly predicting a qualified success. This practice was followed by each teacher in turn. The students were commended, some were criticised but the criticisms were divided, particularly in relation to Ekimov. All, to my satisfaction, unanimously praised Nikolaev as Danforth,

177

though some admitted that he might perhaps be too young for such a figure of authority. The last two people to speak were the elder statesmen of the school, Vitaly Vilenkin and Vladislav Borodinski, the Party leader. First to speak was Vilenkin. Now in his eighties, he had been with the Moscow Art Theatre Company since his youth in the early thirties. In the last years of his life Stanislavski would only communicate with Nemirovich-Danchenko by writing and Vilenkin was given the task of go-between, carrying notes and memos between the two great men.

'As you know, experiments of this kind have been attempted before and particularly in Anglo-Soviet theatrical relations. The last time, the last time it was tried on the stage at the MXAT . . . it was a notable disaster, but now . . . it can be said that this has been a complete and total success. At this time this has been a most important experiment. If our school is to have a future, experiments of this kind must and should continue.'

Then spoke Borodinski. Tall, pencil-thin, elderly, prone to wearing wide-lapel brown denim jackets and jeans with huge turn-ups. I had observed Borodinski over the year, a skulking figure, moving through a haze of smoke and a path of cigarette ash; I had the constant feeling he was eyeing me with deep suspicion. He was the Communist Party leader of the school. He had no function as a teacher but was purely an official responsible for the 'philosophic' welfare and for keeping the inmates of the school toeing the Party line. As he stood up he gave me a sardonic grin. 'As you know, I have been against the whole idea of someone coming from another culture and another ideology to teach our young actors and actresses. It seemed to me to be an utter waste of Party resources. But, I have to say, this is the best thing that has ever happened to this school in the thirty years since I have been here. Like Professor Vilenkin, I believe it must continue.'

Throughout the faculty there was a gasp of utter disbelief as Borodinski made this speech. The man who I thought would probably be my prime opponent had apparently been won over. As he sat down he winked at me. Tabakov beamed.

After the postmortem I asked Professor Vilenkin who the previous notable disaster had been. He sighed and said, 'The notable disaster was Edward Gordon Craig.' That was in 1910.

*

As the final hour of our public opening drew near I became more and more detached from the event. I had been in this position countless times. But here there was an air of unreality throughout the preparations for the first night. My greatest anxiety was about calling home. I now had someone important in my life, someone I could again share excitement with. But I wasn't excited, I simply wanted to call home, to guarantee that there was a world elsewhere beyond Salem and Moscow. The engine that had been driving me throughout the year had shifted into low gear. Success and failure were both indistinguishable and indivisible in their meaninglessness. I was exhausted, a state that I was now bored of. I wanted the whole thing finished. It had been an endurance test fast reaching whatever end it might be, bitter or sweet. It didn't much matter. All that mattered was that I finish the journey at long last.

The feeling on the first night, common to all directors, is of impotence. For me, it was a feeling of blessed relief. As the audience filled the MXAT Studio, I paused to reflect on the odyssey I had made, to think about what I had come through.

The first question was 'Why act?' I act in order to be a receiver and monitor of the human experience. I act in order to re-examine constantly the premises by which I live, premises laid down by my fellow man in which I collude or demur. I act to transmit the philosophy and ideas of the great theatrical thinkers in the ongoing debate of human existence. I act in order to be part of the process of, in Arthur Miller's words, presenting 'man as the creature of society and at the same time its creator'.

At the first stage in the journey of our lives we are all at the mercy of our environment; it conditions us, it colours our response, it prejudices our behaviour and understanding of our fellow man. In the West, we have grown up with a doctrine of cause and effect. The biggest lesson I learnt working in the Soviet Union was that cause and effect simply do not go hand in hand. One and one does not make two: the simplest equation is open to debate. A very hard lesson for a Westerner to understand. The Russian has a Caucasian exterior but his psychological composition is inscrutably oriental. All the time I would judge my Moscow experience by standards of behaviour inculcated in me since birth; behind the Iron Curtain they simply do not apply. What is needed is a tolerance and understanding beyond human endurance . . . Well maybe not quite beyond.

In Moscow a first night at the MXAT is always a major event. Tonight would be no exception. The wife of the British ambassador would be there, plus dignitaries from other embassies. Also in attendance on these gala occasions are the retired actresses from the company, those who have served for over fifty years, wheeled out to fly the company flag. They are the nuns of the theatre who have not lost their youthful optimism and whose love has never faded over the years, the enthusiasts who bring that extra electrical charge to the atmosphere. Again, the major dramatis personae of the past year assembled and passed by in review, this time with their mothers, brothers, fathers, uncles, aunts, sons and daughters.

The lights in the auditorium dimmed to black. The sound of faint bells was heard in the distance, followed by the whispering and giggling of young girls. One by one they appeared, finding their way by candlelight through the darkness. The sounds changed to the evocative beat of a West Indian drum, persistently rising to a pitch before being sliced by the scream of a young girl. The play had begun.

First scene change . . . as smooth as clockwork . . . Someone taps me on the shoulder and tells me that my long-awaited call to London has come through. I make my way out of the theatre towards Tabakov's office to speak to my loved one. As I talk to her, my excitement suddenly returns; I share my feelings of the day and bid her farewell. She will meet me tomorrow evening at Heathrow.

After I put the phone down, I sit for a moment in Tabakov's office and quite suddenly, for no reason begin to cry – a mixture of relief and happiness. I make my way back to the auditorium and climb to the top of the theatre. Looking down on the action of the play below me, I can see both audience and players. The concentration of tension is so palpable one could cut the air with a knife. In the fading moments of the play I return to my position beside Tabakov.

Just at the point where Parris is begging Elizabeth to go to her husband and change his mind, one of the old actresses suddenly leaps to her feet and shouts at the stage, 'Fascist!' followed by another and another.

Tabakov grips my arm and says, 'Look! Look! The play, the play, it is working!'

The curtain lowered; there was a silence which seemed to last for ever. Eventually the actors came on for the curtain call, one by one. Still the silence remained. Then the sound of someone clapping. Within seconds the audience erupted. There were cheers and whistles. Before I knew where I was, I was grabbed by the actors, grabbed by Mashkov and Shentalinski and pulled on to the stage. The cheering went on and on, broken only by Tabakov coming on to the stage and seizing me by the hand. In the tumult I heard him say, 'This is an historic night for our theatre in Moscow. Now we begin to work with our friends in the West.'

After the performance, the stage was cleared and the tables were laid for the first-night party. By past standards of farewell do's this was a very subdued affair, dignified by the weight of what had passed, for all. Brandy and vodka were drunk in equal proportions. This led to the hangover of hangovers. The following afternoon I bade my adieus to those who had become part of my life. It was a hard wrench. I would always be grateful to these young men and women, grateful for what they had given me: my personal *glasnost* and *perestroika*. They gathered round the car to see us off to the airport. It was snowing in Moscow. The car was embedded in the snow. They pushed us on our way, singing the song that they had brought back with them from England, the song that had become the theme of the group, Bobby McFerran's 'Don't Worry, Be Happy'. With this ringing in my ears, we drove off.